Fantasy Baseball for Smart People

How to Profit Big During MLB Season

Jonathan Bales

Table of Contents
Fantasy Baseball for Smart People
How to Profit Big During MLB Season

I. This Is My Intro

> *"Both poker and investing (and daily fantasy sports)*
> *are games of incomplete information. You have a*
> *certain set of facts and you are looking for situations*
> *where you have an edge, whether the edge is*
> *psychological or statistical."*
>
> *David Einhorn*

This is the 11th book in my *Fantasy Football for Smart People* book series. I guess it's now the *Fantasy SPORTS for Smart People* series since, for the first time, I'm writing a book that doesn't have any football content. But yeah, 11 books in a pretty small niche—a reflection of how much time I spend researching fantasy sports, sure, but also a testament to how little of a life I have. One man's lack of social skills are another man's in-depth fantasy sports analysis.

I gained ~~worldwide~~ house-wide fame for my fantasy football analysis, but fantasy baseball is my favorite sport to play. Not season-long fantasy baseball—that shit sucks—but daily fantasy baseball. Not only does the nature of the game and scoring make it exhilarating to follow, but the day-to-day grind can be leveraged into huge profits. NFL for the show, MLB for the dough.

In 2014, I was lucky enough to qualify for the DraftKings Fantasy Baseball Championship in the Bahamas, where I crushed a field of 50 to finish 22nd. Too bad it wasn't a 50/50. I still won a nice chunk of cash for that finish and, luckily, I made some equity swaps that put me on the right side of variance. So that was fun.

If two years ago was a learning period and last season was one for profitability, I think this upcoming season is really a massive opportunity to dominate in daily fantasy baseball. That sentiment really applies to anyone who is willing to put in the time to research and improve. Hopefully this book can be a step in that journey for you.

Like my book *Fantasy Football (and Baseball) for Smart People*, this book is going to be extremely data-driven. Once again, I've worked with DraftKings to uncover what's really winning daily fantasy baseball leagues: which strategies are winning cash games, how to approach tournaments, the optimal salary cap distribution, how much ownership affects win rates, and so much more really cool stuff. I think DraftKings has continually been an innovator in the daily fantasy sports industry, so a big thank you to the guys over there (specifically Rick Sawyer) for being such an integral part of the creation of this book.

- Jonathan Bales, Author of *Fantasy SPORTS for Smart People* and Founder of RotoAcademy

How to Get the Most Out of This Book (Plus FREE CRAP)

Speaking of DraftKings, I have been working with them more and more over the past year. I'm now a DraftKings Pro, and I'm really happy to be able to offer some pretty cool deals to my readers. I think you're going to get a lot of value out of this book, but my goal is of course to convert you into a long-term subscriber. To help do that, here are some bonuses/offers/free crap.

DraftKings

Daily Fantasy Sports for Cash

In addition to a free game, you'll immediately get a 100% deposit bonus up to $600 if you sign up and deposit on DraftKings.

10% Off Everything On My Site (Books, DFS Packages, Etc)

If you want to purchase my Daily Fantasy Baseball Package or any of the books in my Fantasy Sports for Smart People book series, you can do that on my **FantasyFootballDrafting.com**. If you head over there, use the coupon code "Smart10" at checkout to get 10% off your entire order.

Free Issue of RotoAcademy—My Daily Fantasy Sports Training School

Finally, I'm also giving away a free issue—12 lessons—from my daily fantasy sports training school RotoAcademy. I founded RotoAcademy to bridge the gap between the average daily fantasy sports player and the game's elite. My goal is to teach you the tricks of the trade—and give you all kinds of unique data on what's actually winning leagues (like what's in this book)—to help you become a profitable DFS player.

Download the free lessons at RotoAcademy.com/free-download/ or visit RotoAcademy.com/about-faq/ to learn more.

My Daily Fantasy Baseball Philosophy

Sporting events are difficult to predict—even more so on the individual level than the team level—and baseball is arguably the most challenging from day to day. Though there's a ton of consistency in MLB stats over the course of an entire 162-game season (which we can leverage from night to night), it's just damn tough to predict how a player is going to perform in a single baseball game.

If you think about the variance in baseball just from a broad perspective, that idea should be pretty obvious. Even "common" events in baseball, like singles or strikeouts, are still relatively low-frequency; the top batters in the world can barely get a hit in 30 percent of their at-bats.

Further, there's not a huge deviation in players' stats. Only a handful of players have a .300 average each year, yet the league average for batting average typically hovers just above .250. So we're talking about a five-percentage-point difference between an average player and the game's best over the course of an entire season that we need to predict each day.

Don't Run From Variance

But guess what? I don't mind this variance. Actually, I think **the biggest hurdle you must overcome to establish yourself as an elite (and profitable) daily fantasy player is to not only tolerate variance, but to embrace and utilize it.**

That's important is because volatility does not equal unpredictability, nor does it equate to the lack of a competitive edge for daily fantasy players. Let me bold that sentence and type it again: **volatility does not equal unpredictability, nor does it equate to the lack of a competitive edge for daily fantasy players.**

Let me use an example of why I believe this is the case. I got a dartboard for Christmas. I started playing the other day and I'm absolutely awful—like my-wall-looks-like-it-was-in-a-gunfight-with-ant-sized-bullets bad. I was going to go with a Swiss cheese metaphor there but Swiss cheese is just terribly overused as the default there-are-holes-in-something analogy. So yeah, ant-sized bullets.

Moving on.

So I suck horribly at darts. On any single throw, you have little idea if I'm going to hit a triple 20 or throw it into the TV. To say there's a lot of variance in my dart-throwing results is an understatement.

But the other day I was looking at the board and noticed something cool: all of the numbered areas (do those have an official name?) have more or less the same number of holes in them. I actually started to count the total number of holes in each area, and the similarities were pretty incredible. Even though I'm always aiming for the bullseye because I don't know any other games and despite the lack of predictability on each individual throw, there's astonishing consistency over large samples; if I throw 10,000 darts at that board, there will probably be somewhere around 500 throws into each of the 20 areas, assuming each toss has an equal chance of landing in each spot.

Reason No. 1 that volatility doesn't equate to unpredictability: high-variance events can (almost paradoxically) be extremely predictable over the long run. Though I don't have a strong grasp on whether Clayton Kershaw will whiff three or nine batters in his next outing, I can say that he's extremely likely to sit down between 8.0 and 10.5 hitters per nine innings this season—and most likely somewhere around 9.5. The point is that events with a lot of short-term variance and unpredictability can also be very consistent if we give them enough time.

But what about creating an edge? If predicting baseball outcomes is so difficult on the daily level, how is it possible to leverage player performances into profit? The main reason is that **daily fantasy baseball exists as a marketplace**. Sites like DraftKings create player salaries and users pick certain players at different rates. And for the most part, I'm of the belief that **both daily fantasy sites and daily fantasy players react to events that contain a lot of noise as if there's something there that's more meaningful than what exists in reality**.

Ultimately, if you have players priced as if there's less variance than there is, you'll be able to find value. Further, if you have daily fantasy players reacting to those salaries as if there's less variance than there is, then the market will be inefficient (and thus beatable). And **that's really what I believe we have in daily fantasy baseball: a market with wild shifts in price and perceived value that's based on a reality that's probably not quite as up-and-down**.

Just like dart-throwing, it's not like baseball or any other sport is entirely random. So not only can you gain an edge by understanding inefficiencies in the market, but you can also acquire more (or better) information than others to out-predict them, even in the short-term. If you knew that I am slightly biased toward missing the bullseye to the right, for example, that would be actionable information that you could exploit in the same way that knowing that Victor Martinez has almost perfectly equal splits versus lefties and righties.

Cold Streaks

One of the natural outcomes of such a philosophy is that **I'm often bullish on players who aren't playing well of late**, for a few reasons.

One of them is of course pricing. Daily fantasy sites are typically quick to react to recent changes in performance. Sometimes that's smart, like when there's a change in a player's role on an NFL team due to an injury. Baseball is a very binary sport—it's always pitcher vs. hitter with more or less the same parameters in every game—and it isn't as dynamic as some other sports. There are ways that player value can shift (moving up in the batting order, for example), but certainly not to the same degree as most other sports.

If pricing changes too rapidly—at a speed that underestimates variance—using players on cold streaks is a natural extension of that. They might not be ideal in a vacuum, but value effectively equates to expected production minus price. When that price drops too far, it increases usable value.

The second reason I'm often bullish on "cold" players is because their tournament usage will frequently drop. I'm a big tournament player in daily fantasy baseball, for a variety of reasons, and predicting player ownership is a big part of finding GPP success. If buying low on underperforming players also results in lower utilization, that's a really big bonus.

Finally, I'm bearish on very recent stats because I think it's difficult to separate a signal from noise. Do I believe that batters go up to the plate with more confidence at certain times than others or that pitchers can benefit from increased confidence resulting from a previous quality start? I do.

But I also believe it's going to be *really, really* difficult to separate what's "real" in terms of a hot streak from what's just randomness. Maybe a player is hitting well because of specific factors that could help him hit better than normal in the future, but maybe it's just variance. Hitters can be crushing the ball and just get unlucky with placement, or they could be really seeing the ball poorly and still get on base just from dumb luck, and trying to understand hot and cold streaks in a way that's predictive is at best extremely challenging and at worst impossible.

I've always likened this concept to injury proneness. Does it make sense that certain players are more likely to get injured and less likely to heal quickly than others? Sure. We'd never expect two bodies to react to stressors in the exact same way, even on the level of professional sports. But using past injuries to predict future ones is next to impossible because of the variance involved with injuries; we don't know if the data we have is predictive of something to come or just the result of luck.

In the same way we can't properly identify injury proneness, I also think we can't recognize true streaky play—or at least not to a degree that's necessary for the process to be 1) predictive or 2) worth our time.

Game Theory

One of the reasons I think daily fantasy sports aren't capable of being "beaten"—that is, there's no single optimal strategy that will always work—is related to the idea that sports games aren't determined. **The variance ultimately means that you can't act with 100 percent confidence and not only is it smart to question your beliefs and incorporate uncertainty into your decisions, but it's also a vital aspect of becoming long-term profitable**.

To exemplify this, let's assume the opposite—that baseball, for example, is completely predictable. If the game had no inherent variance and we were capable of predicting outcomes with perfect precision, there would be absolutely no incentive to go against the crowd; even if a player were in every single lineup, you'd have no reason to move away from him because doing so would decrease your point total (with 100 percent certainty).

However, we're clearly working with imperfect information here as we can't predict games and player performances with total accuracy. And the level of precision we can actually acquire is a crucial component of determining how much we should seek pure value (placing emphasis on player projections and salaries) and how much we should be contrarian and move away from the herd.

And for the most part, the herd gets things right. When a player is in 50 percent of lineups on DraftKings, for example, it's very likely that he's indeed a quality value. When a player is in just 1-in-100 lineups, he's probably not a sensational value. So in a vacuum, we'd probably maximize projected points by using the highest-owned players each day (if we could predict that…more on that later).

But here's the crucial aspect of daily fantasy sports that I think so many people overlook—and a major reason embracing randomness and employing game theory is so vital: **we're not always trying to maximize projected points**. That's a really vital idea and component of my approach to daily fantasy sports—a keystone to a lot of my philosophies and strategies. **The goal isn't to maximize points, but to maximize win probability (and ultimately profit)**.

Of course, scoring a lot of points is a good thing—you're never going to win an MLB tournament with a score of 80— but points are simply a means to an end; sometimes maximizing projected points is the best way to increase win probability (like in cash games), but sometimes not (like in tournaments).

To hash out this concept in greater detail, here's an article I wrote for some of my subscribers detailing why game theory is so valuable as a decision-making tool:

> *You've been kidnapped and forced to take part in a cruel game that involves guessing at random which of Antonio Cromartie's children I'm thinking of—a boy or a girl. As of the time of this writing, Cromartie reportedly has 12 kids. What is he Catholic? Just kidding Catholics.*
>
> *I can't really find accurate information on the sex of Cromartie's children, but I know he has at least five boys. We'll say he has five boys and seven girls. We'll also say that three of the children are named Jagger, Mar-Qis, and Jerzie, respectively. In reality, two of those names are the kids' real names, which doesn't have anything to do with this game, but wow.*
>
> *So you know that 58.3 percent of the kids are girls and you're asked to randomly guess the sex of the child who is in my head. After one child is used, he/she is eliminated and we move to the next one. What's the best strategy for you to make the most correct guesses?*
>
> *The answer is 'it depends.' It depends on if you're competing with another person. If not, you obviously just want to select the sex with the greatest number of remaining children. That would necessitate guessing 'girl' for at least the first two children. Over the long run, that's the best way to optimize your guesses (in the same way that, if you're trying to pick the most games correctly in the NCAA tournament, you should pick only the favorites).*

However, let's say that you aren't competing alone. Instead, you're facing nine other challengers. The goal isn't to maximize your own success rate, but rather to beat everyone else. Now what's the proper strategy? You can optimize your projected correct answers by using the same strategy as if you were guessing alone, but you can bet that all or at least most of the field is going to use that approach as well.

Knowing that you're competing versus a group of decision-makers just like you, you should actually deviate from the "optimal" choice, at least part of the time. If you were to select 'boy' with one of your first two choices, for example, you'd most likely be wrong. But if you get it right, the payoff would be much greater than if you were to select 'girl' and be correct. Assuming the other nine competitors select 'girl,' you'd immediately gain an advantage over the entire field.

From there, your strategy would be dictated by a number of things, but the point is that doing what's optimal in a vacuum isn't always the best maneuver when you're competing with other minds.

This thought experiment applies directly to tournaments in daily fantasy sports. When competing against hundreds/thousands of other users, there's a major incentive to go off the map and create a unique lineup. It isn't optimal in theory, but in practice, the advantage to be gained is huge.

This can be broken down mathematically pretty simply. Assume you're choosing between a running back projected at 15 points (RB1) and one at just 13 points (RB2). In a heads-up game, for example, you should side with RB1 and his superior projection. There's not much value in being contrarian against just one opponent.

In a tournament, though, it comes down to usage rates. You can't know usage for sure, but let's say that you know RB1 is going to have much higher utilization than RB2. We'll say 40 percent versus 10 percent. If RB1 has a big game—let's say 20 points— you'd gain an advantage over 60 percent of the field, but you'd still need to compete with 40 percent on even footing. Compare that to RB2; if he goes off, you'd need to compete with just 1-in-10 other users on an even playing field.

That difference—a field that's one-fourth the size— suggests RB2 is the superior play unless you believe that RB1 is more than four times as likely as RB2 to give you production necessary to win a tournament; again, we'll call that 20 fantasy points in this scenario.

Now is any running back out there who scores 15 points, on average, four times as likely to go off as one projected to score 13 points? Probably not.

What we need to be concerned with in tournaments isn't just the probability of a player performing as expected, but also the rewards you can reap from being correct.

If RB1 has a 25 percent chance to score big points and RB2 has a 15 percent chance to do it, RB1 would seem to be the better choice. But again, what if RB1's usage is so much higher that it drives down the value of being right? If you have a two percent *chance to win a tournament if you hit on RB1 and a five percent chance to win if you nail your selection of RB2, the latter is the better choice, even though he's less likely to be productive.*

Again, the math: the running backs' value is equivalent to C(P), where 'C' is the chances of hitting their ceiling and 'P' is the probability of winning if they perform at that level. RB1's value would then be 0.25(0.2), or 0.05, whereas RB2's value would be 0.15(0.5), or 0.075. In this scenario, RB2 would offer around 50 percent more usable value than RB1—i.e. a 50 percent greater chance of being in the winning lineup (on a per-lineup basis)—despite being worse value in terms of strict dollars-per-point.

The moral of the story: what's optimal in theory can change when you add competitors. You want to score a lot of points, yes, but the real goal is to maximize the probability of winning. The easiest way to do that in big tournaments is to balance value with low expected utilization.

Another quick example. I was playing Mario Kart the other day (by 'other day,' I actually mean like, no lie, probably 15 years ago) and I was racing a friend to the finish line. I had a choice to drive straight to the finish line (and thus "optimize" my finishing time) or steer slightly to the right to grab a question mark thing. I chose the latter because I figured it would give me a weapon that would allow me to overcome the time lost from going to grab it; in effect, I traded in a bit of time (equivalent to projected fantasy points) in order to increase my edge over my opponent (improving my win probability).

Another way to look at this idea is to consider situations in which you've been trailing in a tournament. When you're in, say, 50th place in a big GPP with two players remaining, it certainly feels a whole lot better if those guys aren't in lineups ahead of you, right? If there are multiple lineups ahead of you with the same players left to go, you have no shot at winning. At that point, you'd certainly trade in those two players for a pair that is unique and gives you a shot at the win, even if they're slightly less valuable, right? Of course. **Being contrarian leads to less fantasy scoring over the long run, but it also gives you more "outs,"** so to speak, in the event that you need to jump other users (which happens almost all the time in a GPP). If pulled off correctly, it can maximize your win probability, which we can all agree is more important than how many points you score.

There are times when we can have our cake and eat it too, acquiring high-value players who are also low-usage. In fact, I'd never recommend being contrarian just for the sake of it, picking off-the-map players with no rhyme or reason. However, the overarching idea is that we need to balance value with usage rates, using game theory to determine which players provide not only the greatest traditional value in terms of dollars-per-point, but also those that offer maximum usable value in terms of increasing the odds of winning.

In short, others' decisions in a marketplace setting are arguably the most important component in determining what's optimal for you.

Antifragility

One of the fundamental aspects of such a decision-making strategy is 'antifragility'—a term coined by writer Nassim

Nicholas Taleb. Something is antifragile if it gains from disorder or "likes" volatility, randomness, or uncertainty. While a mirror is fragile (it breaks when exposed to volatility, such as a fall), the human body is an example of something that's (generally) antifragile. If you lift weights, you have a natural understanding of making something stronger by exposing it to harm. Up to a point, your strength improves when faced with the volatility of lifting weights, which temporarily makes you weaker. Bacterial infections are also antifragile; they're capable of withstanding a surge of antibiotics and coming back stronger than before.

When I qualified for the 2014 DraftKings Fantasy Baseball Championship in the Bahamas, I used an antifragile approach, winning a very large qualifier with a relatively low score of 172 points. That's certainly above-average for a typical league, but below-average for a league of that particular size.

I qualified by stacking a potent offense (the Oakland A's) against a really good pitcher in Madison Bumgarner. Even though that didn't optimize my projected points in a vacuum, I was relatively confident that few users would be stacking Oakland that night (instead on the optimal-in-a-vacuum Rockies at home...much more to come on Colorado). Loaded with power bats, I was willing to take a chance that Oakland would get hot and/or Bumgarner would have an off night. In this scenario, I was willing to trade in some projected points for lower usage, and it worked. The Rockies tanked, a lot of users were hurt, and I benefited from that volatility.

When you fade the Rockies when they're playing at Coors or bypass Peyton Manning in a perceived easy matchup against the Bears, you're basically saying, "Okay, this might not be optimal in theory, but if things don't work out as planned, I'm going to be in the best possible position." That is, **when you're antifragile in daily fantasy sports, you stand to**

benefit from volatility in expected outcomes—that volatility being the highest-owned players/teams underachieving.

Antifragile lineups are inherently more volatile than others. Because you benefit so immensely when the crowd is wrong but also get hurt so badly when the crowd is correct (since you have an entire pool of users that will pass you), results tend to be extreme with a contrarian approach; Ricky Bobby would be proud, because you're generally either first or last (or close to the extremes, anyway). I tested my MLB tournament results against a normal distribution and I indeed finished very close to the top or very close to last in way more leagues that you'd expect from chance alone. That's a good thing in GPPs.

Again, an antifragile approach is inherently tied to game theory, the value of which stems from some level of unpredictability. Basically, we're using other players' rationality against them. It's a completely rational tactic to play the top values because they're going to ultimately maximize fantasy scoring. But when a mass amount of users employ the same plan, there's a potential edge to be had if the popularity of that strategy surpasses the probability of them being right.

Note that one of the prerequisites of being antifragile in daily fantasy sports is having the psychological makeup to lose more frequently than you win. I'm not ashamed to admit that, as primarily a GPP player, I don't profit most days. And by employing a tactic that purposely bypasses value in many situations, I profit even less frequently than I could if I stuck with the chalk. In 2014, for example, I was profitable just 24 percent of the time. I was profitable less than twice per week! But, when I cashed, I finished in positions that were much higher than you'd expect from a random distribution.

How frequently you win is just one piece of the puzzle, with the other being *how much* you win when you win and *how much* you lose when you lose. **An antifragile tournament player is okay with losing small amounts of money on a semi-consistent basis because, when he strikes, he usually strikes big**.

Malcom Gladwell wrote a really nice profile of Taleb and his antifragile approach to options trading at Empirica:

> *One of Taleb's earliest Wall Street mentors was a short-tempered Frenchman named Jean-Patrice, who dressed like a peacock and had an almost neurotic obsession with risk. Jean-Patrice would call Taleb from Regine's at three in the morning, or take a meeting in a Paris nightclub, sipping champagne and surrounded by scantily clad women, and once Jean-Patrice asked Taleb what would happen to his positions if a plane crashed into his building. Taleb was young then and brushed him aside. It seemed absurd. But nothing, Taleb soon realized, is absurd.*

> *Taleb likes to quote David Hume: "No amount of observations of white swans can allow the inference that all swans are white, but the observation of a single black swan is sufficient to refute that conclusion." Taleb has constructed a trading philosophy predicated entirely on the existence of black swans, on the possibility of some random, unexpected event sweeping the markets. He never sells options, then. He only buys them. He's never the one who can lose a great deal of money if G.M. stock suddenly plunges. Nor does he ever bet on the market moving in one direction or another. That would require Taleb to assume that he understands the market, and he doesn't. He hasn't Warren*

Buffett's confidence. So he buys options on both sides, on the possibility of the market moving both up and down. And he doesn't bet on minor fluctuations in the market. Why bother? If everyone else is vastly underestimating the possibility of rare events, then an option on G.M. at, say, forty dollars is going to be undervalued.

So Taleb buys out-of-the-money options by the truckload. He buys them for hundreds of different stocks, and if they expire before he gets to use them he simply buys more. Taleb doesn't even invest in stocks, not for Empirica and not for his own personal account. Buying a stock, unlike buying an option, is a gamble that the future will represent an improved version of the past. And who knows whether that will be true? So all of Taleb's personal wealth, and the hundreds of millions that Empirica has in reserve, is in Treasury bills. Few on Wall Street have taken the practice of buying options to such extremes. But if anything completely out of the ordinary happens to the stock market, if some random event sends a jolt through all of Wall Street and pushes G.M. to, say, twenty dollars, Nassim Taleb will not end up in a dowdy apartment in Athens. He will be rich.

What Empirica has done is to invert the traditional psychology of investing. You and I, if we invest conventionally in the market, have a fairly large chance of making a small amount of money in a given day from dividends or interest or the general upward trend of the market. We have almost no chance of making a large amount of money in one day, and there is a very small, but real, possibility that if the market collapses we could blow up. We accept that distribution of risks because, for fundamental reasons, it feels right.

In the book that Pallop was reading by Kahneman and Tversky, for example, there is a description of a simple experiment, where a group of people were told to imagine that they had three hundred dollars. They were then given a choice between (a) receiving another hundred dollars or (b) tossing a coin, where if they won they got two hundred dollars and if they lost they got nothing. Most of us, it turns out, prefer (a) to (b). But then Kahneman and Tversky did a second experiment. They told people to imagine that they had five hundred dollars, and then asked them if they would rather (c) give up a hundred dollars or (d) toss a coin and pay two hundred dollars if they lost and nothing at all if they won. Most of us now prefer (d) to (c). What is interesting about those four choices is that, from a probabilistic standpoint, they are identical. They all yield an expected outcome of four hundred dollars. Nonetheless, we have strong preferences among them. Why? Because we're more willing to gamble when it comes to losses, but are risk averse when it comes to our gains. That's why we like small daily winnings in the stock market, even if that requires that we risk losing everything in a crash.

At Empirica, by contrast, every day brings a small but real possibility that they'll make a huge amount of money in a day; no chance that they'll blow up; and a very large possibility that they'll lose a small amount of money. . .“We cannot blow up, we can only bleed to death,” Taleb says, and bleeding to death, absorbing the pain of steady losses, is

precisely what human beings are hardwired to avoid.
"Say you've got a guy who is long on Russian bonds,"
Savery says. "He's making money every day. One
day, lightning strikes and he loses five times what he
made. Still, on three hundred and sixty-four out of
three hundred and sixty-five days he was very
happily making money. It's much harder to be the
other guy."

Before moving on, here's a look at how a typical antifragile
approach to daily fantasy baseball GPPs might affect one's
bankroll over the course of one month.

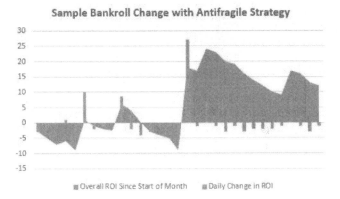

In this example, there were only six profitable days out of 31,
yet the overall ROI for the month was +12 percent. Such a
plan of attack trades in frequent small losses (the result of
generally forgoing some level of value that's well-known by
the public) for infrequent but very sizeable profits (the result
of benefiting from volatility, i.e. standing to gain when the
public is either inaccurate or on the wrong side of variance).

Summing Up My Approach

Much of my approach to daily fantasy sports—particularly baseball—centers around embracing uncertainty and trying to put myself in a position to not only not be harmed by it, but also to benefit from it.

A big part of that comes down to understanding that I probably don't know as much as I think I do. I think it's pretty natural for people to act with certainty about their beliefs, and sometimes that's beneficial; the underdog that thinks they can win a game they otherwise probably wouldn't win is the type of self-fulfilling prophecy in which strong belief, even if irrational, leads to success.

For our purposes, though, ignoring uncertainty and volatility can be harmful. **If we never account for the fact that we could just be wrong, we're creating a fragile system that opens itself up to being harmed by variance.** That's one reason that traditional projections and values can be very misleading; if you think you can consistently project a difference of 10.0 fantasy points for Player X and 10.2 fantasy points for Player Y, you're going to get yourself into trouble. It's fine to make projections, but it's vital to incorporate uncertainty and the consistency with which we can trust them. "Here's what I think this player will do, but how confident can I be that I'm right?"

And the more uncertainty, the less value there is in following the herd—one reason value matters more in basketball (a game in which players have a narrow range of fantasy outcomes on a nightly basis) than baseball (a game in which the daily fantasy outcomes are distributed over a very wide range). The more variance, the more we can benefit from using game theory (depending on the league type) as a path to creating an antifragile plan of attack.

None of this is to say that I believe baseball or any sport is totally random, or even mostly random—it's not like I could go out there and hit dingers—but rather that there's just more variance than most people would like to admit. As I mentioned, that limits the importance we can place on short-term data, but it increases the importance of uncovering long-term signals.

Basically, the more variance, the more we can predict numbers to regress toward the mean. Figuring out that "mean"—whether it's league-wide or on the level of a single player—is key. If I'm projecting Adam Wainwright's strikeouts per nine innings this year, for example, it's important to know that he had only 7.1 last year after four straight seasons above 8.0, but it would also be useful to know how pitchers at his age typically perform relative to their previous peak production. Maybe pitchers normally don't see a major decline in strikeouts until age 35, for example, in which case Wainwright could be in for a positive regression.

Thus, a big part of what I do is try to get my hands on as much aggregate data as I can get—much from DraftKings, much collected on my own. I want to know the timeless (or at least semi-timeless) sort of information: how left-handed finesse pitchers age compare to right-handed power hurlers or exactly how valuable it is to play at Coors Field, for example.

The numbers allow me to develop general heuristics that I think make for a nice daily fantasy decision-making foundation. I hardly follow such heuristics at all times—there are plenty of occasions when it's smart to deviate from the rule—but in general, I think it makes sense to have aggregate data as a backbone.

Again, this relates back to variance and our inability to consistently and accurately identify exceptions. In the NFL, for example, there's a very low success rate for running backs who check in slower than about 4.50 in the 40-yard dash. Are there times when it's acceptable to draft a running back who runs a 4.55? Sure. It's not like those guys *never* succeed. But teams consistently miss on those sorts of players because identifying the traits that might allow for a player to be an exception to the rule is really challenging, and overall, data has shown NFL teams would be better off drafting running backs based off of a single naïve heuristic—faster is better—than whatever voodoo they've been using in the past.

I think we can have the best of both worlds: data-driven heuristics and logical, subjective decision-making. Actually, the heuristics act as a foundation from which we can make smart subjective decisions and adapt as daily fantasy players. That evolution is key.

My goal is to take as scientific of an approach to daily fantasy sports as I possibly can. I want to create falsifiable theories, test them, and alter my opinions when necessary. I want to use data to inform my decisions, implementing heuristics as a foundation and stats as a path through which I can improve my subjective decision-making. I want to constantly adapt to new information.

But most of all, I want to use what I find to help you do the same—teaching you how to become a fisherman instead of just giving you a fish—so that you can transform into a dominant, profitable daily fantasy player for the long haul.

A Daily Fantasy Sports Glossary

DFS players have a language all their own. My friend CSURAM88 once said, "The GPPs overlayed and the payouts were super flat, so I was really +EV. I faded Arizona and stacked Colorado because I was bullish on the Rockies at home, and I ended up seeing 5x on my investment because Tulo is the GOAT."

If you have no idea what this means, don't worry. Before we get into the good shit, here's a DFS glossary for you to check out if you're new to the game. I use a lot of terms throughout the course of the book, so feel free to check back here if you come across something that's unfamiliar.

+EV

Positive Expected Value; a situation in which you expect a positive return on your investment. Daily fantasy players are constantly searching for +EV situations.

$/Point

Dollars per point; the number of dollars you must spend (in cap space) for every point a player is projected to score. A lower $/point is preferable.

50/50

A league type in which the top half of all entrants get paid and the bottom half lose their entry fee. 50/50 leagues are generally considered safe, but they can become dangerous if you enter the same lineup into multiple leagues.

Bankroll

The amount of money you're willing to invest in daily fantasy sports

Barbara Walters Game

Courtesy of Al_Smizzle, a game/performance that was "obvious" with 20/20 hindsight

Bearish

A pessimistic outlook on a particular player, team, or situation. If you're bearish on a player, you wouldn't use him in your lineups.

Bullish

The opposite of bearish; an optimistic outlook on a particular situation. If you're bullish on a player, you'd use him in your daily fantasy lineups.

Buy-In

The amount of money needed to enter a particular league

BvP

Batter versus Pitcher; a batter's history against one particular pitcher

Cash Game

Usually considered any league that pays out at least one-third of entrants (50/50s, heads-up games, and three-mans)

Ceiling

A player, team, or lineup's upside; the maximum number of points they could score

Chalk

The most obvious plays; the players who clearly offer a lot of value and will be highly owned

Commission

The fee charged by the daily fantasy sites to play in a league; typically around 10 percent of the total buy-ins

Confirmation Bias

The tendency to search for or confirm information that fits with preexisting beliefs

Contrarian
To go against the grain—the opposite of "chalk"

DFS
Acronym for daily fantasy sports

Dong
A home run, a.k.a. dinger

Donkey
A bad DFS player; someone who is -EV

Exposure
The amount of money invested in a player; if you have a lot of exposure to a particular player, it means you have a relatively high percentage of your bankroll placed on him.

Fade
To avoid a particular player or game, i.e. "I'm fading the Rockies game because I think the teams will be really highly owned."

Fish
The same thing as a donkey; a poor player

Floor
A player, team, or lineup's downside; the minimum number of points they could score

Freeroll
A daily fantasy league that's free to enter but has cash prizes

GOAT
Greatest of All-Time (in opposition to WOAT)

GPP
"Guaranteed Prize Pool"; a league in which the prize is guaranteed, regardless of the number of entrants

Head-to-head (Heads-Up)
A one-one-one daily fantasy league

Hedge
Actions taken to reduce the overall risk of your lineups; if you're excessively bullish on a particular lineup, for example, you would hedge by creating other lineups without any of the same players, even if it's sub-optimal. When you hedge, you're reducing risk at the cost of also reducing upside.

High-Low
Also known as "stars and scrubs"; when you select multiple elite, high-salary players to accompany low-priced, bargain bin players (in contrast to a balanced strategy)

Late Swap
To edit your lineup on DraftKings after a contest has started; you can edit players whose games have not yet begun

Lock
A must-play

Multiplier
A league in which you can multiply your entry fee by a certain factor based on the payouts; in a 5x multiplier, for example, the winners get paid out five times their entry fee. The higher the multiplier, the more high-risk/high-reward the league.

Narrative
A widely accepted explanation for a particular phenomenon, whether true or not; a "revenge game" is a type of narrative

Nuts
The best possible lineup; similar to "the nuts"—the best possible hand—in poker

Overlay

When a daily fantasy site loses money on a GPP; if $20,000 is guaranteed but there are only $18,000 worth of entrants, the overlay is $2,000.

Pivot

To move away from a player you previously had in your lineup; if you liked Troy Tulowitzki and he's scratched, you could pivot to a shortstop with a similar price tag.

Player Prop

A Vegas line that projects a particular stat for an individual player

Punt

A calculated, low-priced risk at a certain position used to save money elsewhere; if you go min-priced at second base, for example, you'd be punting the position so you can load up on studs. Punt plays lead to high-low lineup construction.

Qualifier

A league in which the winners don't receive cash, but rather win a "ticket" into another league; a 10-team qualifier with a $12 buy-in might give away one ticket into a larger league with a $100 buy-in, for example; in opposition to cash games

Reach

To select a player who doesn't provide great value, i.e. a high $/point; reaches typically result in -EV (negative expected value) situations

ROI

Return on Investment

Shark

A really good DFS player

Splits

A player or team's stats broken down into different categories; ex: lefty/righty splits

Stacking

To pair multiple players from the same professional team in an effort to increase upside; stacking is particularly popular in daily fantasy baseball

Sweat

Watching games with a lot on the line; ex: I was in first place in a huge GPP and sweating the final game of the night.

Tilting

To develop stress or anxiety from game outcomes that often leads to sub-optimal decision-making

Train

Entering the same lineup into one league multiple times (only advisable in qualifiers)

Whale

A high-volume DFS player (whether good or bad)

A Few Notes

As you might have noticed, certain sections/sentences of the book are bolded; these represent the most vital points/concepts from each section. If you're reading this somewhere quiet—like in a church or library—and you find that my writing is too hilarious to handle, you can just skip to those bolded parts to understand the central ideas.

At the beginning and end of each chapter, you'll also find quotes. These are VERY IMPORTANT WORDS that I've collected by Googling things like "quotes on randomness" and "best quotes about baseball." Take these very seriously and DO NOT skip over them.

Finally, at the end of most chapters, you'll find a section called "CSURAM88's Analysis," complete with relevant thoughts from Peter Jennings—the No. 2 ranked daily fantasy sports player in the world. CSURAM88 won the DraftKings $1 Million Fantasy Baseball Championship in 2014—the same one for which I qualified—and at the time of this writing, he has over $10 million in gross earnings on DraftKings.

So yeah, he knows what the fuck he's talking about.

CSURAM88's Analysis

He's right. I know what the fuck I'm talking about.

"I know what the fuck I'm talking about."

CSURAM88

II. Perfecting the Process: How (and What) to Research for Daily Fantasy Baseball

"How you climb a mountain is more important than if you reach the top."

Yvon Chouinard

All of the data in this book is geared toward helping you make better choices when picking players and fielding lineups on DraftKings. I'm a huge proponent of implementing objectivity, even if it's just as a foundation for subjective decision-making.

At the end of the day, though, you need a method with which you can quickly process data in an actionable way. One of the primary benefits of playing daily fantasy baseball is that it's truly a daily sport, which is awesome for maximizing your ROI. But it also means there's a limited amount of time to research, particularly because a lot of important factors—like the weather, lineups, and Vegas lines—aren't static.

Thus, developing a research routine is a really, really important aspect of being a profitable daily fantasy baseball player. You need to know where to go, which data to consider, which factors aren't all that important, and how to utilize new information.

I don't think there's one perfect process by any means—you can find all sorts of valuable stats and analysis all over the web—but there are certainly a few key pieces of information that you'll need to uncover each day. So here's a look at my particular process for daily fantasy baseball research—which factors I consider and where I visit to get that information.

Weather: Daily Baseball Data, Forecast.io

In most sports, weather is either irrelevant or only a mildly significant factor in projecting players. Not so in baseball. **The weather matters in baseball, and it matters a lot.**

I start my weather research at Daily Baseball Data. **The first thing for which I'm searching is the probability of rain** in any open-air stadium without a retractable roof. If you use a player in a game that rains out, you're shit out of luck. It's a massive risk to roster anyone in a game with a significant probability of rain.

In cash games, I'll almost never use a batter in a game with around a 30 percent or higher chance of thunderstorms. If there aren't thunderstorms on the horizon—just rain—then that's a different story because baseball games are rarely cancelled from rain alone with no lightning.

When it comes to pitchers, my threshold for usage is even lower than 30 percent. Because such a huge chunk of your fantasy points come from your arms—and because they're the most consistent source of points you can acquire—you'll be in big trouble if you take a zero from a pitcher. On top of that, whereas rain delays don't really hurt batters because they stay in the game, starting pitchers are almost always pulled following a delay.

You can take more chances in GPPs, especially if you're fielding multiple lineups. If you think the public is going to completely fade a game because of rain, it can sometimes make sense to be bullish on that contest in a tournament. That's the sort of antifragility we're always seeking in GPPs;

the game might get rained out, but if it doesn't and you stack a team that goes off, you're in a position to really capitalize on that volatility.

When a game looks like it might get rained out, I check that city's forecast on Forecast.io. Daily Baseball Data allows you to visualize every game at once, but Forecast.io is more accurate because it aggregates a bunch of different services: AccuWeather, the National Weather Service, and so on. I'm a really big advocate of a "wisdom of the crowd" approach to making predictions, and Forecast.io uses that methodology to maximize accuracy.

Other Weather Factors

Rain is just part of the equation when it comes to predicting baseball outcomes. **I use weather factors perhaps more than any daily fantasy baseball player** I know—weather is a massive component of my MLB model—**and the four primary factors I consider are temperature, wind (speed and direction), humidity, and air pressure**.

Let's work in reverse order. Anyone who has watched a game at Coors Field in Colorado knows that air pressure is of massive importance when projecting batters. Playing a mile above sea level, the Rockies and their opponents benefit immensely from low air density in the area, which results in reduced friction on a baseball as it travels. My mom hasn't picked up a baseball bat a day in her life, but I'd be willing to bet she could hit a ball out of Coors.

Coors Field is an extreme example—one I'm going to study in greater depth later because it's so interesting—but it follows that we should be monitoring air pressure in other cities if we're trying to determine hitter-friendliness in a given matchup.

Further, air pressure also affects the path of pitches, too. Researchers at the Sloan Sports Analytics Conference found that **certain types of pitchers—namely those who throw a high percentage of breaking balls—perform best in conditions with low air density. Fastball pitchers exceed expectations on high air density days. Ideally, you'd like to use batters hitting in low air density against fastball pitchers.**

Humidity is another important factor in projecting the flight of a baseball, but one that goes overlooked. When humidity is high, it reduces the friction between a baseball and the air, ultimately aiding it in traveling farther. **All other things equal, we want as much humidity as possible**, assuming it isn't accompanied by precipitation.

If you've ever monitored the Vegas lines when there are windy conditions at Wrigley Field, you know how much wind speed can affect the flight of a baseball. Many times, Vegas won't even offer a run total for the Cubbies when they're at home and the winds are gusting. When they do, it isn't uncommon to see the projected run total jump by 25% or more, which is pretty insane.

Of course, **it's important to compare the direction of wind to a particular stadium's orientation**. If the wind is gusting out to centerfield at 20 mph, that's much different than if it's blowing straight in. The wind direction doesn't affect the baseball solely after it is hit, either. Take a look at the average final pitch speed (as it crosses home plate) versus wind speed in different directions.

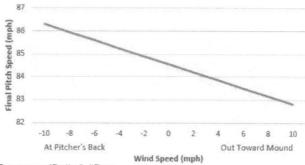

Final Pitch Speed vs Wind Speed

*Data courtesy of The Hardball Times

There's a strong correlation between pitch speed and offensive stats—it's obviously more challenging to hit faster pitches—and pitchers can throw the ball a whole lot faster if there are strong winds at their back.

The final atmospheric condition to consider is the temperature. **Temperature has a profound impact on air density; the higher the temperature, the lower the air density and the farther a baseball will travel**.

To help quantify the effect, I charted the runs scored per team since 2000, broken down into six temperature buckets.

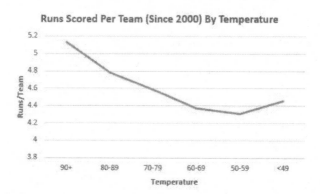

When the temperature was very hot—over 90 degrees—teams scored around 13 percent more runs than when the temperature was between 70-79 degrees and 18 percent more runs compared to when the temperature was between 60-69 degrees. That's a pretty substantial jump based on a factor that a lot of daily fantasy baseball players don't even consider.

As I'll show later, a big part of having success on DraftKings is about predicting home runs. If you want to do that with the greatest possible accuracy, it's imperative to give yourself exposure to games being played in hot weather.

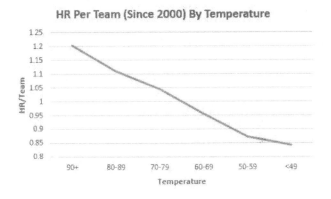

Since 2000, teams playing in 90-plus degrees have gone deep 26 percent more often than those playing in temperatures of 60-69 degrees and 38 percent more frequently than those playing in temperatures of 50-59 degrees. As Jesse Katsopolis would say, "Have mercy!"

Putting It All Together with Da Weather
Part of the puzzle when it comes to improving as a daily fantasy baseball player is equipping yourself with the data

you need to gain an edge, but just as important—perhaps more so—is being able to leverage that information to turn a profit. You can have all of the stats in the world, but they're useless if you can't use them in an actionable manner to improve your predictions.

I've backtested the importance of each aspect of weather when it comes to projecting fantasy production. **In my Daily Fantasy Baseball Package, I provide bottom-line values for each game to help you understand and visualize weather factors in a very simple way. I also combine this research with the Vegas lines and other factors (more to come on those) to help you predict offensive upside, who to stack, which pitchers are safest, and so on.**

Even if you don't purchase the package, make sure you're monitoring all components of the weather—not just precipitation—when deciding who to play in a given day.

Lineups: RotoGrinders

One of the challenging aspects of MLB research is that lineup cards typically don't come out until a couple hours before the first pitch, and sometimes even later. For the most part, that's not a massive hurdle when it comes to researching because 1) you can generally predict most lineups with decent accuracy—the same studs almost always play—and 2) you'll always have knowledge of a team's lineup prior to their game starting, so you can make adjustments.

I use RotoGrinders to monitor MLB lineups. They have each team's batting order once the lineup cards are in, as well as a bunch of relevant information, such as weather, Vegas lines, predictive stats, and so on.

There are a few things to consider when looking out for lineup cards. The first is of course the batting order. Most players hit at the same spot in the order each day, but some don't. When a batter moves from the back of the order to the No. 2 spot, that's a significant jump. With more projected plate appearances and the benefit of hitting close to his team's sluggers, a player's outlook can completely change based on that rise in the order.

I did some research on plate appearances and historic DraftKings points (using the current MLB scoring system). Here's a look at those figures for each spot in the lineup...

In terms of bulk points, **No. 3 hitters have historically scored more fantasy points per game than any other hitters**, including leadoff guys. I'd argue that the No. 2 through No. 5 hitters on most teams are superior to leadoff men, but the No. 1 hitters have the benefit of accruing more plate appearances over the course of a season, and that's valuable.

I rearranged this data to show how each spot compares to the peak performers (No. 1 hitters for plate appearances and No. 3 hitters for fantasy points)...

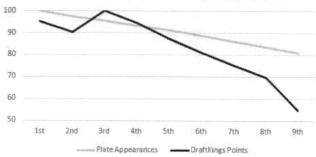

You can see that No. 8 hitters typically have around just 84 percent of the plate appearances of leadoff hitters. When a batter who normally hits late in the order makes a move up for a game, that jump should be reflected in the value you place on him.

Also note that it seems like **there's a pretty big drop-off in production at around the No. 6 batter**; that's probably the point where the hitters 1) are getting worse and 2) have little opportunity for a lot of plate appearances.

Another thing to consider with the lineup is how lefties and righties are distributed. Lefty/righty splits are a really important part of projecting MLB players, so it's of course imperative to know how many lefties a particular southpaw will be facing in a given matchup, for example, and how he performs against lefties in general relative to right-handed batters.

Even though you'll always have access to a team's lineup card prior to their game beginning, that doesn't mean you'll always have perfect knowledge of all lineup cards when daily fantasy baseball contests begin. Since some West Coast games can start three-plus hours after daily fantasy baseball leagues start, you might need to work with limited information at times.

However, this can be leveraged into an advantage if you play it properly. I'm going to have a lot more awesome data on West Coast games and player usage, but on DraftKings, you can start any player in a late game without hesitation since the site has a late-swap feature, i.e. you can swap out any player whose game has not yet started for any other similar player.

The late-swap feature not only opens up a lot of game theory elements and other additional strategies, but it also allows you to leverage others' fear of missing lineup cards into an advantage; if you start a hitter on the Dodgers and he gets scratched, you can always swap out so you're never really getting screwed over by MLB lineup changes.

Vegas: Bovada

The best companies in the world do a really nice job of outsourcing tasks that increase the overall efficiency of the company while aiding in improving their bottom line. If we're thinking of ourselves as the CEOs of daily fantasy baseball prediction companies, then it makes sense that we should spend as little time as possible on things that we can have others do for us.

Wouldn't it be amazing if there was some sort of entity out there that had all kinds of money riding on the outcomes of sports games and individual player performances and was thus incentivized to make really accurate predictions that we could basically just steal?

Oh, there is? Yeah, there is: Vegas.

Vegas accounts for basically every relevant factor when they set their spreads, totals, and props. They've proven to be extremely accurate in the past. There's an amazing section on the Vegas lines and their practical uses in daily fantasy sports in my book *Daily Fantasy Pros Reveal Their Money-Making Secrets*. That discussion could lead to an entire book itself, but one of the central points is that, while Vegas cares about public opinion, their first aim is to create an accurate line. If they do that, they'll limit their downside and maximize long-term profits.

The Accuracy of Vegas

For us daily fantasy baseball players, it really comes down to one question: can the Vegas lines help us make more accurate predictions? And that answer, without a doubt, is yes. We have the best oddsmakers in the world weighing weather, ballpark factors, pitcher matchups, recent performance, and lots of other factors. When they predict that the Cowboys will score 24 points or that the Rangers' median projection is five runs, that's highly likely to be very close to reality. There's all sorts of data that I've collected in various sports showing how accurate Vegas has been.

Even if you consider what Vegas offers to be "common sense"—an argument I've heard from a number of people who somehow have decided to forgo leveraging their apparent ability to beat Vegas into huge profits—**there's no doubt that we can increase our efficiency by stealing Vegas's predictions.**

I liken this to a company outsourcing work that they can get completed cheaply and more efficiently than what they could do on their own. So why in the world would you run through all of the work of considering 100 different inputs that might affect a baseball team's run projection when you can get that information immediately from a highly reliable source? Even if you were just as accurate—and you likely aren't—it still wouldn't make sense to not take that sort of data for free. The cost—a couple minutes of your time—is basically nothing, yet you can receive all sorts of incredibly useful insights.

At this point, I think it's important to confirm that Vegas is not only accurate, but also a reliable tool for daily fantasy players. So I looked at the overall fantasy production for teams in games projected at eight runs, then compared that to other run totals.

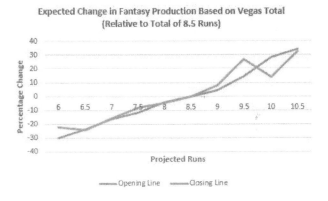

There's a very clear, linear relationship here; **games projected at six runs by Vegas have historically seen between 20 and 30 percent fewer fantasy points than those projected at eight runs**—depending on if we use the opening or closing line. On the other end of the spectrum, **games projected at 10.5 runs have witnessed around 33 percent more fantasy points than those projected at eight runs**. Those are pretty sizeable differences, eh?

I also charted the reliability of using the Vegas lines as a direct proxy for fantasy scoring. Here's a look at how the change in run total has historically compared to the change in fantasy production.

Using Vegas Total as a Proxy for Fantasy Points

Actual Change ————— Expected Change (Using Opening Line)

Up until the 9.5-run mark, fantasy production has been directly linked to the Vegas lines—an almost perfectly linear correlation. What's really interesting is that actual fantasy production jumps considerably over what we'd expect once hitting the projected 10-run mark, i.e. if you targeted teams in games projected at 10 or more runs, you would have seen a sizeable jump in fantasy production over games at just 0.5 fewer projected runs.

I'm not entirely sure why this is the case. It could just be that teams with really high projected run totals also have far more upside than others. Maybe 10.5 runs is the median projection for a specific game, but the high-upside offenses in that sort of contest have the ability to occasionally erupt for 20-run sorts of contests that throw off the overall numbers.

Either way, two things are true:

1) We can trust the Vegas lines to help project players in daily fantasy baseball.

2) When possible, we should target hitters in games with a high projected total.

Leveraging the Lines

There are three useful numbers that Vegas can give us in baseball: the total, the moneyline, and props. The total is the projected number of runs for both teams combined. The moneyline offers odds of each team winning. Props are individual predictions of a particular player or team's performance.

There are generally moneylines associated with the totals and props in MLB which change the odds. RotoGrinders has a really useful Vegas page that auto-calculates everything for you, showing you how the spreads and moneylines ultimately affect each team's projected run total.

Those projected run totals are really useful in daily fantasy baseball, particularly if you plan to stack an entire offense. If you want to use six batters on the White Sox, for example, the Vegas line will be really important in deciphering your lineup's upside. If Vegas has Chicago projected at 5.2 runs and you're using two-thirds of their offense, that total is going to be strongly linked to your fantasy production.

I also use the projected run totals to target pitchers. Baseball is obviously zero-sum such that the success of a pitcher is directly related to the lack of success for an offense; **when Vegas has a particular team projected really poorly, it's a good sign that the opposing pitcher will perform well**. The moneyline is important, too; when a particular team is a big favorite to win, the starting pitcher for that squad also has a high probability of getting fantasy points for a win.

The overarching idea here is that Vegas can and should be a very fundamental part of your daily fantasy baseball research process. In an extremely short amount of time, you can identify which teams are likely to win, how much they're likely to win by, and (with player props) which players are the best bets for elite fantasy production.

Splits (L/R, wOBA, ISO, xFIP, SIERA, K/9, Park Factors): FanGraphs

By looking at the weather and Vegas lines to start my research process, I'm trying to get a really broad sense of which teams/pitchers might have the most upside in a given day. Part of the reason that I do that as opposed to first looking at individual players is because, as I'll explain later, I generally stack batters from the same team, even in cash games, which means that a top-down approach to research is probably best for me.

Still, this is an individual game, so it's vital to be able to sift through a vast amount of data for every available player. In terms of individual player research, I start with lefty/righty splits. **The difference in how players perform based on handedness can be drastic**. Here's a look at OPS—On-Base Plus Slugging—for the top 150 batters since 2000.

OPS Splits Since 2000 (Top 150 Hitters)			
	LHP	RHP	Difference
LHB	0.738	0.846	0.108
RHB	0.894	0.811	0.083

You can see that **right-handed batters as a whole are better against lefties than righties, while lefty bats are much, much better against right-handed arms than southpaws**. It's vital to understand how a batter or pitcher's handedness and matchup will affect his performance in a given day. I typically use FanGraphs to easily sort through this data.

I always want to have the most exposure to the players with the most favorable splits. Though that typically means playing batters against pitchers of the opposite handedness, that's not always the case. Some guys are "reverse splits" players, some perform equally well against both hands, and so on.

For pitchers, handedness still matters a lot, specifically in situations in which they'll face a lineup with an unbalanced handedness of hitters. Managers often shake up their lineups to account for the handedness of the opposing starting pitcher, so sometimes you'll get a southpaw facing an entirely right-handed group of hitters, which is of course generally less ideal (from the pitcher's viewpoint) than going up against a balanced lineup.

So handedness splits are probably the most important factor I consider, but we still need specific numbers to analyze. For me, those stats are wOBA (Weighted On-Base Average) and ISO (Isolated Power) for hitters and xFIP (Expected Fielding Independent Pitching) and K/9 (Strikeouts Per Nine Innings) for pitchers.

wOBA

Weighted On-Based Average is a Sabermetrician's dream because it's a really nice catch-all statistic that does a nice job of capturing overall offensive quality at the plate. wOBA is basically a superior On-Base Plus Slugging. OPS does a good job of combining both power and the ability to reach base, but it doesn't weigh certain achievements in the proper way according to how much they're worth to an offense. wOBA corrects for that, providing a really accurate representation of a hitter's ability.

As with every stat I analyze, I care about wOBA splits—not overall wOBA. Some hitters have well above-average wOBAs against righties but can't get a hit to save their life against southpaws, for example, and I want to know that.

Daily fantasy sports sites like DraftKings do a pretty good job of pricing players according to their *overall* quality, which leaves room for us to find inefficiencies in that pricing based on splits. If Player X is priced at $5000 because he has an overall wOBA of .350, that pricing might be accurate in a vacuum, but we'd still be overpaying for him against lefties if he has a .320 wOBA against southpaws (and thus underpaying for him versus right-handed arms, against whom his wOBA would be higher than .350).

In 2014, Andrew McCutchen led all batters in wOBA at .412. A .400-plus wOBA is elite territory—only six players surpassed the mark in 2014—and anything above .340 or so is really good. The league average has dipped over the past decade, for obvious reasons (fucking global warming, am I right?), but .312 or so is about average league-wide.

ISO

ISO—Isolated Power—is a very simple metric that calculates raw power by dividing extra bases by at-bats. I like to use ISO because so much of daily fantasy baseball success, especially on DraftKings, comes down to giving yourself as much access to dongs as you can get. Never thought I'd type that sentence. To win a big GPP, for example, you're gonna need some dingers, and ISO will help you deliver those. Typically, I'll be more inclined to use wOBA in cash games, but some combination of wOBA and ISO for GPPs.

And again, everything is broken down by handedness. I don't care about overall ISO numbers—just ISO splits.

The league-average ISO is right about .135. The Rockies unsurprisingly led all teams in ISO in 2014 at .169, and Edwin Encarnacion led all batters at .279. Anything above .200 is a quality ISO number, while anything below .100 or so is poor.

While ISO and wOBA do a really nice job of capturing the majority of what you need to win, they're not the only pieces of the puzzle. Neither metric accounts for stolen bases, for example, which can be a really large part of increasing your upside and safety in daily fantasy baseball.

Typically, **I have one general rule of thumb when selecting batters: if he doesn't have the ability to either go deep or steal a bag with regularity, then I don't want to use him**. Baseball is too volatile of a sport to rely on someone who hits for average, for example, since they still have big downside (zero points is realistic for any player in any game), yet don't offer you very much upside.

xFIP

Let's move to the mound, where one of the most popular catch-all statistics—the wOBA for pitchers—is xFIP (Expected Field Independent Pitching). **xFIP is a derivation of FIP, which calculates what a pitcher's ERA would look like if he had normal results on balls that are put into play**. The idea is that pitchers don't have much control over what happens once a ball is hit, so FIP attempts to remove the "luck" and provide a number that's more predictive of future ERA than past ERA.

xFIP adds another layer by also calculating how many home runs a pitcher should have allowed based on his fly ball rate—something that generally regresses toward the mean. So in effect, we're trying to calculate what a pitcher's ERA *should* look like based on how he's pitched, attempting to account for the randomness of batted balls.

I like to exploit this when a pitcher's xFIP is much different than his ERA. Earned Run Average is such a commonly used statistic and a big component of his DraftKings salary. **When a pitcher has an ERA of 3.00 but a xFIP of 4.40 early in the year, for example, that's a sign that he's probably going to regress, and thus could be overvalued**.

Clayton Kershaw led all pitchers in xFIP in 2014, and it wasn't close; his 2.08 xFIP bested second-place Felix Hernandez (2.51) by a wide margin. The league average xFIP is typically around 3.75 or so. Anything around 3.15 is great, while anything approaching 4.30 is considered poor.

SIERA

SIERA—Skill-Interactive ERA—is another statistic that attempts to quantify what a pitcher's ERA "should be." It's quite similar to xFIP, except it also accounts for differences in balls put into play.

An average SIERA is around 3.90. Anything below 3.00 is excellent, while anything above 4.50 is poor. Want to guess who led baseball in SIERA last season? Yes, Kershaw; his 2.09 SIERA bested Hernandez (2.50).

The reason that I bring up both xFIP and SIERA is that people have different views on batted balls and the randomness surrounding them. SIERA tries to adjust for expected differences in pitchers' batted ball profiles. What's important to me is that **SIERA has proven to be more predictive than xFIP for basically every meaningful pitching stat**.

The calculations for xFIP and SIERA are quite similar, so as long as you're using one of them to spot discrepancies between perceived and actual performance (and ultimately value on DraftKings), then you'll be ahead of the curve.

K/9

While xFIP and SIERA capture a pitcher's overall ability very well, it doesn't directly account for strikeouts. And if you're playing daily fantasy baseball on DraftKings, you need to target high-strikeout pitchers. I'm going to show you some correlations on the individual stats that are most connected with winning daily fantasy baseball leagues, but the strongest one (by far) is the link between pitcher strikeouts and 50/50 wins. **The correlation between strikeouts and winning cash games is so strong that you could make an argument that the majority of your daily fantasy baseball research time should be allocated to predicting strikeouts for pitchers**.

K/9 simply calculates the number of strikeouts a pitcher records per nine innings. It's not the only metric that matters—someone like Stephen Strasburg has a really high K/9 but often doesn't pitch a lot of innings—but K/9 is a major piece of the puzzle. And since it's somewhat independent of xFIP, you can use the two in conjunction without much overlap (as opposed to wOBA and ISO).

Ballpark Factors

All of these stats of course need to be adjusted for the opponent—it doesn't really matter if a guy has a decent wOBA if he's a lefty facing Kershaw, for example—but you also need to consider ballpark factors. Certain parks are of course more hitter-friendly than others.

At times, it can be difficult to separate the team from the park. I think where a lot of the numbers on ballpark factors fail is not properly adjusting for team strength. How much of the Rockies' offensive success has been due to playing at Coors Field, for example, and how much has been due to them just being a quality offense?

To quantify this, I charted the percentage of a team's total bases they tallied at home. This is a pretty simple concept, but the idea is that **1) total bases are a decent proxy for overall offensive quality and 2) if a team plays in a very hitter-friendly ballpark, we'll see a larger percentage of their offensive production come at home**.

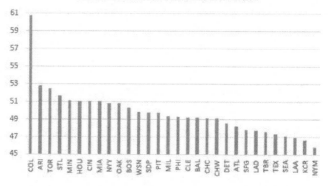

Pct of Total Bases at Home in 2014

Uh, yeah, hi, holy shit.

In 2014, only one team saw more than 53 percent of their total bases come at home. It was Colorado at nearly 61 percent. That's just insane.

Though there are a lot of games played during an entire MLB season, there's still some variance here, so I charted the same stats from 2011 to 2014.

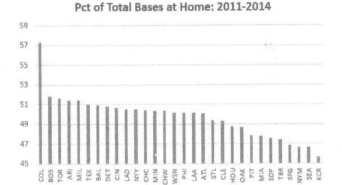

Pct of Total Bases at Home: 2011-2014

The Coors Field effect isn't quite as strong, but the results are still staggering.

Since 2011, the five teams with the most hitter-friendly parks have been Colorado (by a mile), Boston, Toronto, Arizona, Milwaukee, and Texas.

The five squads with the least hitter-friendly parks have been Kansas City, Seattle, New York Mets, San Francisco, and Tampa Bay.

These numbers are important, but we can still look at ballpark factors according to handedness; some stadiums are known to be friendlier to lefties than righties, for example. FanGraphs has good data on park factors by handedness.

Analysis: Fantasy Insider, DraftKings Playbook, FantasyPros, Hardball Times, BaseballHQ

I perform all of the aforementioned research—looking at weather, checking lineups, researching splits, weighing ballpark factors, and crunching other numbers—before I ever look at anyone else's analysis. I think this is a really important aspect of being a profitable daily fantasy sports player; **when you start to get sucked into the herd mentality, you ultimately start to lose your edge**. It's easy to second-guess yourself and reverse course because others don't agree with your opinions.

Not that second-guessing yourself is bad. It isn't. In fact, I'd argue you should second-guess every decision you make. That's really what this is all about: questioning your most basic beliefs, testing everything, and evolving as a player.

Ultimately, I think it's shrewd to consider others' views, assuming you're *supplementing* your own research and not *replacing* it. When someone you respect likes a player you also like, it can boost your confidence in that selection, maybe even increasing the amount of exposure you want to have to him. On the other hand, when a few smart guys I trust don't like someone I previously thought was a good value, I'll take another look; I'll probably still use that player, but I might limit my overall exposure as a way to hedge against perhaps an increased probability of being wrong.

Some of the sites that offer analysis I trust, in addition to those already mentioned (RotoGrinders and FanGraphs, for sure), are Fantasy Insiders, DraftKings Playbook, FantasyPros, Hardball Times, and BaseballHQ. Again, I think it's really important that you formulate your own opinions, but it certainly helps to utilize others' work when appropriate.

When I'm reading others' work, I'm looking for viewpoints I might have missed, particularly in the form of objective data. If Analyst X says "I don't like Andrew McCutchen tonight," I don't really give a shit. If he says, "I don't like McCutchen tonight because he has just a .120 ISO off of right-handed pitchers who induce a high fly ball rate," then that would matter to me.

My Daily Fantasy Baseball Package

One of the tasks I'm trying to accomplish with my Daily Fantasy Baseball Package (available at FantasyFootballDrafting.com) is to give players a quick look at all of the relevant information they need in a given day: weather, splits, Vegas lines, stacking information, and so on.

I'm basically giving subscribers a glimpse into my research for each day of the MLB season—which pitchers I like, which hitters make for great tournament plays, which teams I'm going to stack. I think you'll find that it will 1) help you get inside of my mind to see which direction I'm headed and 2) provide the tools you need to make quality lineups on your own.

Independent Research: Baseball Reference, FanGraphs, SaberSim.com

One of the challenging aspects of playing daily fantasy baseball is the day-to-day grind. Sure, you can take days off whenever you need them, but who the hell wants to do that!? Not when big money is up for grabs.

Most of your research time will go into uncovering the best plays and creating the optimal lineups for a given slate of games. However, I always try to set aside time to perform broader research projects. Unlike physicist/wannabe famous person Neil deGrasse Tyson, I don't think philosophy is a "useless endeavor," but rather the foundation of intelligent scientific and mathematical theories. Albert Einstein used to think logically about the way that the universe "should be" based on what he observed, then sought out to find the math behind his conceptions—not the other way around.

I want to take a very scientific approach to daily fantasy sports because I think it's the only way to grow as a player, but we need to make sure we're asking the right questions. We don't need to know if the ball makes a sound when it hits the bat if no one is in the stands to hear it—assuming there isn't a batter, I actually think it doesn't since sound is a mind-dependent quality, but whatevs—but we do need to make sure that we're at least moving in the right direction when we head deep down these different rabbit holes of data.

With that said, I believe it's important to take a step back and ponder how all of your beliefs fit with one another and, public opinion aside, how much they're data-driven versus narrative-driven. Is it okay to punt the pitcher position? Is stacking really a high-variance strategy in baseball? Is it okay to pay for home run hitters in cash games?

Much of this book is an attempt to answer those overarching questions for you, but certainly I think **it's always worth your time to question basic assumptions—including those proposed in this book**—to ultimately ensure you're improving as quickly as possible in daily fantasy sports. If you want to perform independent research, here are some good sources for data to help you complement the 'what' with the 'why.'

Baseball Reference Play Index

This is it. This is the Holy Grail of baseball research. I used Baseball Reference's Play Index for so much of the research in this book. Whether you want to find something as broad as the league average wOBA over the past three years or something as specific as how well 23 to 25-year old left-handed hitters have hit for power in division games, you can locate that data with the click of a few buttons.

IT'S AWESOME.

FanGraphs Spray Charts

FanGraphs is the leader in MLB analysis for a reason; they have the ultimate combination of data, tools, and analysis. Most of it is geared toward traditional baseball and not daily fantasy baseball, but there's a ton of overlap, too.

One of the really useful tools they have is a spray chart generator. You can set different parameters for hitters, pitchers, ballparks, and so on to see where balls have historically been batted.

When I'm undecided on a player, I might look at his spray chart to determine if his batted ball tendencies match up well with the particular park in which he's playing.

SaberSim.com

Finally, SaberSim.com is a unique way to project baseball players on a daily basis. You can use various projection systems and run a bunch of different simulations to generate projections for players and teams.

SaberSim understands each player's handedness, ISO, wOBA, matchup, and so on, so it can produce numbers that represent the probability of certain occurrences. While I don't care much about individual player projections in MLB, I use this tool as a way to help predict the home run upside of offenses that I want to stack.

No Projections?

There are a variety of sites out there that project players in every sport, including baseball. **I personally do not create projections for MLB players**. That is true on the level of both individual stats (like singles, doubles, etc) and total fantasy points.

The reason I don't project players in that way is because of what I discussed in the intro: randomness. **Baseball is so volatile from night to night that we just can't place too much confidence in projections; such a system would be extremely susceptible to measurement errors**.

When I discussed antifragility, I explained that it's always in our best interest to develop systems and methods that benefit from chaos. That's the idea behind being contrarian in tournaments; when others are wrong—when there's volatility—you reap the rewards.

Well, a traditional projection system or dollar-per-point calculations for baseball are extremely fragile; very small events can dramatically change their accuracy. If a player is 1-for-4 in a given game, for example, and then hits a towering would-be home run that's robbed by the centerfielder, he was literally inches away from a big night hitting .400 with a dinger. Instead, he was 1-for-5 and probably didn't help you much.

Baseball is such a binary, event-based sport that there can be massive swings in player value due to very small, even random happenings. Maybe that centerfielder got laid that morning and was on his 'A' game. His sexual habits might have ultimately cost you a tournament victory; that might be a $20,000 swing based on something you clearly can't predict.

Compare baseball to a sport like basketball, where projections can be very practical and useful. There's variance in the NBA too, but players score points in a much more linear way; LeBron James might go for 20 points in a night or he might score 40 points, but he's very unlikely to score two or four or even 10.

Baseball, on the other hand, is completely non-linear, and that makes it difficult to project. Again, that doesn't mean it's any more challenging to beat than other daily fantasy sports—perhaps just the opposite—but it does ultimately increase the fragility of traditional stat projections.

To be clear, **I don't think stat projections are completely useless** because they'll force you to consider factors that are important—like wOBA and ISO and whatever—**but you can probably find more efficient ways to spend your research time than trying to figure out if you should project Josh Donaldson at 0.29 or 0.32 home runs**.

And Batter vs Pitcher Data?

When I asked some of my readers what sort of topics they wanted me to cover in this book, BvP was far and away the No. 1 item. Naturally, I'm going to spend a few paragraphs on it and then we aren't going to talk about BvP ever again. K?

Okay, here's the deal: I think it's natural and probably accurate to assume that certain batters perform better off of particular pitchers than others. **Whether it's the mechanics of a pitcher's throwing motion, the type of pitches he throws, or whatever, we'd certainly expect some batters to crush certain pitchers and struggle versus others, even over the long run**.

But there's a difference between a particular phenomenon existing and being able to use it to make accurate predictions. At the end of the day, I don't really care how a particular batter has performed in the past—we don't get fantasy points because Miguel Cabrera spanked the ball *last* week—I just care about predicting what's going to happen in the future with some degree of accuracy.

I think data and a scientific, mathematical approach to daily fantasy sports is the best way to do that, but not all data is the same. Side note: Lots of people who work with data use the phrase "data are…" Literally no way I'm ever writing "data are."

Anyway, just because analytics can help us make money in daily fantasy sports doesn't mean all numbers should be treated equally. For the most part, **all we care about is that certain numbers can help us make more accurate predictions, and when it comes to BvP, there's no data that suggests it has any predictive value for projecting hitter performance**.

When it comes down to it, the sample sizes involved with BvP are almost always too small to draw meaningful conclusions; we can explain past events well, but not use the data to help us moving forward. As a batter accrues more and more at-bats against a single pitcher, we can become more and more confident that the results we've witnessed are representative of reality. The problem is that the point at which we can be semi-confident in BvP numbers is probably somewhere in the range of 100 or more plate appearances—a figure almost no one reaches against a particular pitcher.

Ultimately, **it's just very, very difficult to separate BvP from variance**. Of course we're always going to see a wide range of performances for a batter against different pitchers, but for the most part, it will be challenging to know if those results are a signal of something greater, or just noise.

So do I use BvP data? Almost never—maybe a couple times per season. **There are two occasions when I believe maybe, just maybe, we can use BvP data as a *minor* component of our decision-making**.

The first is when a hitter has truly extreme results against a particular pitcher. The matchup that comes to mind when talking about outlying results is Paul Goldschmidt against Tim Lincecum. At the time of this writing, Goldschmidt has 28 at-bats against Lincecum with 15 hits, seven home runs, 17 RBI, 1.357 slugging percentage, and 1.916 OPS.

Goldschmidt's results are so extreme that, even though they could be the result of chance, it's probably more likely that he truly has Lincecum's number. And by that, I mean he'll probably continue to crush him in the future, albeit not to that degree. And again, almost all BvP data isn't extreme enough to overcome small sample sizes.

The second time that I consider using BvP data is when analyzing a pitcher, specifically when a pitcher faces a group of hitters against whom he's thrown a lot in the past. Maybe he has 30 career matchups against one guy, 35 against another, 20 against another, and so on. **In isolation, we can't be confident that the data from those individual matchups**

is meaningful, but in aggregate, it might be actionable because we can overcome the sample size issue.

I still don't use BvP data much for pitchers, but when I do, it's typically for in-division games. In those games, a pitcher might have enough collective matchups against the opposition's hitters that we can start to get a sense of whether or not his past numbers are indicative of future play. But again, the sample size needs to be large and the results still pretty extreme, in one direction or the other.

Bringing It Together

The most important part of my daily fantasy baseball research routine is acquiring as much relevant information in as efficient of a manner as possible. Part of that efficiency comes via a routine, as I use the same sources and pretty much the same general process each day.

One of the potential traps of such an approach is continuing to do the same thing, again and again, even if it isn't working. I think testing your results and refining everything you do— even if you're winning—is a crucial part of remaining profitable over the long run.

I personally like to use the weather and Vegas lines/props to create a shortlist of batters and pitchers that I want to target. I really focus on the team level a lot more than in other sports since teammates' production is so intertwined in baseball. Unlike in basketball—a sport in which teammates almost always cannibalize one another's fantasy upside—players on the same MLB team often move in unison. That's due to a synergistic effect in scoring (if your batter hits a grand slam and you rostered everyone who is on base, too, YOU SCORE ALL THE POINTS), and also the fact that teammates of course face the same pitchers; if a starting pitcher comes out flat, the entire offense stands to benefit.

I'm also extremely bullish on lefty/righty splits, so every decision I make is a reflection of that. Every other stat I analyze—wOBA, ISO, K/9, xFIP, and so on—is broken down by handedness. I think daily fantasy sports sites often formulate salaries that don't account for handedness splits, or at least not as strongly as they should.

Once I've completed my research, I seek the opinions of a few analysts I trust. Their projections/values/plays/thoughts won't necessarily change mine, but they might alter the level of confidence I have in certain guys, which helps me determine the overall exposure I want to each player or team.

And lastly, if you're ever undecided on what to do, just select a group of players you like and let your girlfriend or wife pick who to play. You could have all the stats and insight in the world, but nothing is as accurate as your significant other's intuition.

Just ask her.

CSURAM88's Analysis

There's no component of MLB research that's bigger than studying the Vegas lines. The odds are actually the first thing I study when preparing for a day of daily fantasy baseball. I go to Pinnacle Sports to look at the lines because they update them quickly and accurately.

For batters, I consider a team's projected total—particularly for stacking an offense—as well as individual player props. Vegas is going to be right more often than pretty much anyone, so it would be crazy to not consider how they feel about each player/team in a given day. The run totals and props are really the foundation of my hitter research for MLB.

For pitchers, I care about a few different numbers out of Vegas. One is the moneyline—specifically how likely it is that a pitcher will throw well and get a win—and I *really* care about line movement. More so than in any other sport, I study Vegas line movements intently for baseball; when the moneyline moves a lot—say from -150 to -190—that's an obvious sign to study the pitchers in that game. When the line moves in favor of a pitcher, I generally want to target him, and vice versa if the line moves in the opposite direction.

Vegas's strikeout props are also really important for me, especially when you consider how valuable strikeouts are on DraftKings. The great thing about the props are that they factor in projected innings, matchup quality, weather, ballpark, and everything else you need; it's just a bottom-line number that's really, really useful when projecting my arms. Plus, whereas not every batter will have a prop available, Vegas usually has props for every starting pitcher.

Once I finish with my Vegas-based research, I consider individual stats. Jonathan hit on the major stats that I consider—wOBA and ISO for hitters, especially. Those numbers are important for batters who don't have props offered by Vegas.

Finally, I adjust everything for weather, particularly if there were recent changes. If the wind starts blowing out at Wrigley, for example, that's a really big thing that Vegas can't capture with their opening lines—so I adjust all of the research Vegas gave me to account for any recent changes in weather.

As far as rain is concerned, I'm extremely risk-averse with my pitchers. I play mainly cash games, so I don't need to hit a home run with every pick. If there's any chance that a pitcher is in a game that could get delayed because of rain, I won't play him in cash games.

I'm more risk-seeking when it comes to my bats. I still won't play a hitter in a game that could get rained out in my cash-game lineup, but a delay doesn't matter very much (and could actually help if the opposing starting pitcher gets pulled).

In tournaments, I'm still risk-averse with my arms, but I'll take on more risk with my hitters. I like to stack teams in games that actually have a chance of getting rained out. If there's a 50 percent chance of thunderstorms in a game that's otherwise a really favorable spot for hitters, for example, I'll sometimes stack that game because I know people will be scared away by it. That's something that's obviously not advisable in cash games.

"Research is formalized curiosity. It is poking and prying with a purpose."

Zora Neale Hurston

III. Cash Games vs Tournaments: How to Win Different League Types

"Never think that lack of variability is stability."

Nassim Nicholas Taleb

Most of you are total degenerates like me, so I'm going to assume you've sat down at a blackjack table or two at some point during your life. If so, you're familiar with the dealer offering you insurance when he/she could potentially have blackjack.

And you presumably always say no because the math isn't in your favor. The house is taking a little bit more than you'd lose over the long run if you just play out the hand. That's how insurance works, so from a strict EV standpoint, it's never "worth it" for you to have insurance. The casinos and insurance companies need to make money somehow, right?

But that doesn't mean all insurance is bad. Most people are in agreement that some form of health insurance is a positive. Why? What's different between health insurance and insurance in blackjack?

Well, the downside of losing one hand of blackjack is 1) known, with the money already being wagered and 2) not very large. Now compare that to health risks, which can be unknown and substantial in nature. You can go bankrupt from a serious health problem, but, unless you use a David Choe style blackjack play, you don't possess the same type of downside from a single hand of blackjack.

Health insurance works not because it is +EV, but because it substantially limits your risk or ruin. Because of that, it's worth it to "overpay" for some types of insurance, to an extent, because you can reduce the fragility of your wealth and overall wellbeing.

A similar phenomenon exists in daily fantasy football, where many shrewd users pay top-dollar for quarterbacks in cash games, even if those players aren't the best values in terms of strict dollars-per-point. The reasoning for that is because quarterback is the most consistent position in football, paying for an elite passer can almost act as an insurance policy; it helps to increase the floor of your lineup, with the hope being that it outweighs any reduced upside (the result of technically forgoing some level of value).

Improving DFS Win Rates

I'm a really big believer that you can improve your NFL profitability simply by understanding weekly variance and structuring your lineup in a way that reflects what you want to accomplish. Specifically, you should be trying to widen or narrow the range of potential outcomes for your team, dependent on the league type in which you're participating.

The numbers show that allocating a high percentage of your DraftKings salary cap to quarterbacks and running backs, for example, can help you win cash games. Those two positions are the most consistent, so by spending big for production on which you can count, you're narrowing the window of possible scores for that lineup.

To demonstrate why that's smart in cash games, here's a (completely hypothetical) sample probability of NFL scores on DraftKings.

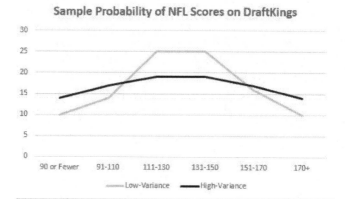

The goal in cash games is to produce lineups that will take down the average lineup as often as possible. That means that cash game success comes down to giving yourself as much exposure as possible to above-average scores—which is different than trying to score as many points as possible.

In the sample probability of NFL scores, you can see that the odds of scoring 111+ points with a low-variance approach (paying for quarterbacks and running backs, not stacking QB-WR, etc.) are much greater than with a high-variance approach; even though the probability of an elite score is superior with a high-variance approach, the chances of turning in a cashing score are much better by playing it conservatively—by taking out "insurance" on your downside. It might appear as though the low-variance approach has a more drastic range of outcomes, but it doesn't; there's a higher probability of a narrow range of quality results in the 111-150-point range.

In the case of football, a low-variance cash-game approach works because the value of limiting downside outweighs that of maximizing points and/or upside.

I don't think the same is true in MLB. I believe daily fantasy baseball scoring is completely asymmetrical in a way that dramatically favors taking a high-variance approach and seeking upside, even in cash games. That is, the benefits of taking on some risk far outweigh the costs.

To demonstrate that, here's another sample distribution of scores, this time representing MLB.

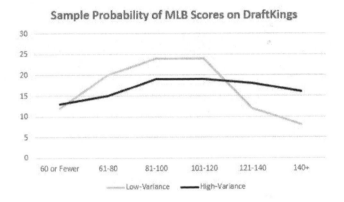

Sample Probability of MLB Scores on DraftKings

In terms of true downside, the high-variance approach (which might include stacking teammates, paying for home run ability, and other strategies I'll discuss in a bit) is still just slightly worse than the low-variance approach; the odds of an abysmal score with the high-variance lineup are slightly increased.

There's also a wider range of outcomes with the high-variance approach here, just like in NFL; the odds of scoring between 61 and 120 points, for example, are 68 percent with the low-variance strategy (in this example) and just 53 percent with the high-variance method.

In this example, though, the upside produced by the high-variance approach far outweighs the downside. If you're looking to score a shitload of points to win a GPP, the high-variance option is clearly superior and gives you far more access to those elite scores. But, BUT, in terms of scoring a modest amount of points (we'll say 101 or more, which is around what you need to beat MLB cash games long-term), the high-variance approach is STILL better—access to that 101-plus range 53 percent of the time, compared to just 44 percent for the low-variance tactic.

Due to the way that MLB fantasy scoring is distributed—which has very much to do with the fact that it's an event-based sport with highly volatile results—I think we need to change our thoughts regarding when and when not to seek variance.

I guess now is the time that I should give you some data to help prove my case.

True or False with League-Specific Strategies

To do that, I'm going to play a little true/false game with a few statements regarding cash game/GPP strategy, all of which I'd say the general public believes to be accurate. Using my research and data from DraftKings, I'm going to attempt to either confirm or dispel these notions.

1. You should pay up for pitching in cash games: TRUE

There are a variety of ways that we can analyze the merits of a specific approach to daily fantasy baseball, two of which I believe can greatly enhance our understanding of league-specific strategies.

The first is to study player and stat consistency. The reason that quarterbacks have so much more consistency than wide receivers from game to game is because the former have a more sizeable sample of relevant plays (maybe 35 passing attempts versus a handful of targets for pass-catchers). The same is true in baseball; pitchers have way, way more opportunities than batters to "show their stuff," so it makes sense that they'd have a higher level of consistency and predictability

The same idea holds within the pitcher position, too; since pitchers typically approach or surpass triple-digit throws in a given game, it's more challenging for a bargain-bin arm to outperform an ace than it is for a min-priced shortstop to outperform Hanley Ramirez, for example.

And remember, the more randomness, the more we should be looking to save money. If outfielder production were theoretically completely random, we should never pay more than the minimum price for any outfielder; there just wouldn't be any incentive to do so.

On top of that, **the primary stat that DraftKings rewards heavily for pitchers—strikeouts—is also one of the most consistent on the seasonal and nightly levels**; the same pitchers are the ones who continually whiff the most batters, and those elite arms tend to cost the most money. FanGraphs has a really cool correlation tool showing that the strength of the correlation between strikeouts in Year Y and Year Y+1 is around 0.71. Compare that to just 0.31 for ERA.

The second way to determine if it's intelligent to allocate a high percentage of cap space to pitchers is to see if such a strategy has led to success in the past. That's why all of this DraftKings data is so cool; it gives us a "glimpse into reality," so to speak. We can make all sorts of hypotheses about what *should* work in different league types, but at the end of the day, the historical daily fantasy results are what matter most.

For example, even though strikeouts are the most consistent pitching stat and even though it makes sense to pay for consistency in cash games in theory, the pragmatic value of such a strategy depends on DraftKings' pricing. If they were to jack up the prices of high-strikeout arms too much, we might have a really good theory that ends up being useless in practice.

So, without further ado, here's a look at the typical salary cap allocation for cashing versus non-cashing 50/50 lineups on DraftKings...

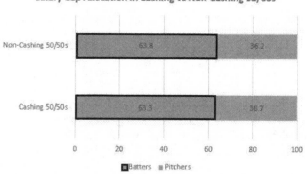

The historic data confirms the idea that **successful cash lineups allocate a higher percentage of their cap space to the pitcher spot than unsuccessful lineups**. The difference of 0.5 percentage points is small, but significant over a sample of 10,000-plus leagues. For reference, 0.5 percent of the salary cap on DraftKings is equivalent to $250.

2. You should punt pitching in tournaments: FALSE

There are really two distinct schools of thought when it comes to GPP pitcher selection. Some people are firm in their belief that you should always pay for the best pitchers, while others argue that you should be willing to roster a low-priced arm in tournaments.

Like most issues, I'm somewhere in the middle on this one, but I'd say I'm probably leaning toward still paying top-dollar for elite arms in GPPs. There are a variety of reasons for this.

The first is that, **though I'm what many consider a contrarian GPP player by nature, I'm not really willing to go against-the-grain as much at pitcher**. That's due to the nightly consistency, along with the types of offenses I typically utilize; I like to "underpay" for cheaper stacks with upside, then go big with my pitchers and "other" batter spots. Every day is different and that's not a firm, no-matter-what strategy, but it's usually where I find myself.

Plus, the data once again supports the idea of paying up for arms in all league types…

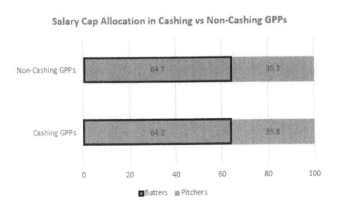

Salary Cap Allocation in Cashing vs Non-Cashing GPPs

	Batters	Pitchers
Non-Cashing GPPs	64.7	35.3
Cashing GPPs	64.2	35.8

Again, the difference is 0.5 percentage points. Note that winning GPP lineups have spent less on pitching than winning 50/50 lineups, but I think that's just a reflection of daily fantasy players as a whole being more willing to punt a pitcher spot in tournaments, which drags down the overall allocation. The important part here is that **successful GPP teams are spending more money on pitching than GPP lineups that don't cash**.

I'm going to have some other really cool data on balancing value with ownership in both the batter and pitcher selection chapters that I think will provide even more evidence that, even if you're trying to be contrarian in large-field GPPs, pitcher isn't the place to do it.

3. Stacking is smart in tournaments, but not cash games: FALSE

Even if you haven't looked at daily fantasy baseball statistics a day in your life, you don't need to play the game for very long before you realize the benefits of stacking players in tournaments. It's very, very clear that using hitters from the same team improve your lineup's outlook.

Looking at some data from my book *Fantasy Football (and Baseball) for Smart People*, I charted the probability of scoring 150 or more points on DraftKings with X number of teammates in your lineup.

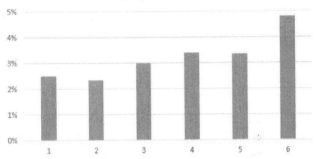

Yes, there's more that goes into GPPs than scoring a lot of points, but it's not like you're going to win any tournaments with a score of 90; you still need to seek upside, and there's a very clear relationship between stacking and maximizing your ceiling.

Stacking gives your lineup upside, but how much does it increase downside? Well, it depends on the number of teammates you stack...

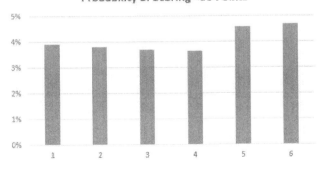

Historically, **stacking three or four bats has been *less* volatile than not stacking at all**! It's only once we hit the five-player

mark that stacking has been risky, and even then, the downside is minimal.

From these numbers alone—dramatically increased upside with only slightly greater risk—I think we can conclude that stacking isn't necessarily a bad idea in cash games. Do I always stack three/four bats in my head-to-head and 50/50 leagues? No, but I certainly don't avoid it, either.

To confirm this idea, here's a look at the probability of scoring 90 points on DraftKings…

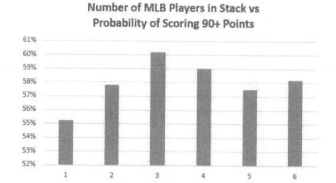

And a look at the odds of crossing the 110-point mark…

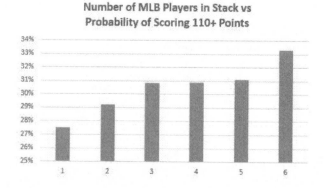

I don't think there's a whole lot of doubt left here. While stacking a bunch of players from the same team might be just a tad riskier than not stacking, the improved upside more than makes up for the added volatility.

Not only is stacking in heads-up and 50/50 leagues not a poor idea, but it looks as though it might be the most underrated tactic you can use to improve your cash-game win rate.

4. You should look for power in GPPs, but the ability to get on base in cash games: FALSE

The degree of consistency and predictability inherent to a sport is directly related to how you should balance risk and reward. **Baseball—with its lack of day-to-day predictability and asymmetrical payoffs (meaning risk-seeking strategies provide a higher level of benefits than harm)—is a sport in which the data points to taking on more risk than in other sports, including in cash games.**

When it comes to targeting specific stats, I think there's somewhat of a consensus that you should be more willing to pay for power in GPPs than in cash games, and I disagree with that idea. For one, every hitter has the same floor of zero points, yet some (home run hitters and base-stealers) have remarkably more upside than others.

Even if we ignore the numbers, logically it just doesn't make sense to use a player who doesn't have a high ceiling when every player's floor is zilch. Even though cash games are generally about maximizing exposure to above-average scores, which is related to reducing volatility, it's not like more upside is ever a poor thing; more upside is only a negative when it's accompanied by an equal or greater amount of risk. We do indeed see asymmetrical scoring in daily fantasy baseball, but in the other direction, allowing for the ability to take on massive upside with only a pinch of extra risk.

On a day-to-day basis, getting on base (via hits, walks, or whatever) is a more frequently realized skill than hitting dongs, which has led a lot of people to believe that they're improving their outlook in cash games by targeting "safe" players who score fantasy points primarily from just getting on base. Maybe their floor is just ever so slightly higher than a high-strikeout power hitter, but is it worth gaining an extra point on a floor if it means conceding 10 points off of your ceiling?

A lineup filled with contact hitters who don't steal bases is fragile; you're still taking on risk because baseball is volatile in general, yet you're also forgoing the ability to benefit from relatively low-frequency events (home runs and stolen bases).

Further, remember that volatility and randomness can be quite predictable over large samples. Relying on a single power hitter to go deep is high-variance; relying on a team of eight of them to do it, not as much.

Volatility also experiences a smoothing out quality over time such that, if you're continually giving yourself exposure to home runs, you'll inevitably get them. Plus, home run rate is actually one of the most consistent stats for batters.

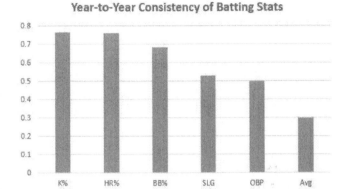

While a player's batting average fluctuates pretty much from season to season, home run rate does not. Players who go yard (and those who strike out) do it on a consistent basis.

This point is related to the final reason I think you should emphasize power, even in cash games: home runs are relatively scarce. Scarcity is one of the driving forces in determining value in any marketplace. **The guys who hit home runs on a consistent basis don't only hit home runs— it's not like Giancarlo Stanton doesn't hit single and doubles, too—so the batters who can't give you dingers offer a skill that's highly replaceable**.

5. You should maximize expected points in tournaments: FALSE

Buckle up motherfuckers, because you're about to get what I consider to be one of the coolest pieces of data I received from DraftKings. BTW, I just tried to find a synonym for 'motherfuckers' because I wrote that and was like, "Hmm...I can't really use motherfuckers in this book, can I?" BUT MICROSOFT WORD HAS NO SYNONYMS FOR

'MOTHERFUCKERS.' So now it's in the book four times instead of one.

Okay, here's the first part of the data, which deals with ownership percentages and GPP success.

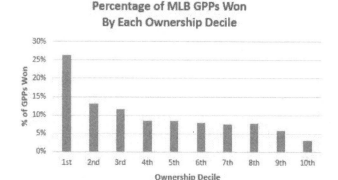

In terms of ownership, the data is sorted into 10 equally sized deciles. That means we're looking at the cumulative ownership of every lineup in a tournament, then sorting it into 10 equal buckets.

If things were totally random, we'd expect each decile to win 10 percent of GPPs. In reality, only three deciles have surpassed that win rate, due primarily to the very high win percentage from the lineups with the highest-owned players.

What does this tell us? It tells us that **the daily fantasy baseball market is at least somewhat efficient because the most popular players are performing the best. Going into any tournament, odds are that a "chalk" lineup—one with the most popular players—is going to win**. That's just the nature of the beast since 1) the chalk is by definition the most abundant type of lineup and 2) the highest-owned players are also usually those who offer the most value.

BUT, that's not the end of the story. The most important thing to keep in mind here is that **the chances of a chalk lineup (or any type of lineup) winning a GPP aren't the same as the odds of *your specific lineup* winning if you use highly owned players**.

Remember, **your goal is to not only score a lot of points, but also to put yourself in a position to battle with as few people as possible so that you can maximize the benefit of scoring so many points**. If you roster the Padres a lot, for example, you'll be in a really strong position if they go off. I'm not necessarily telling you to do that because San Diego sucks, so **you're always trying to balance expected player usage with value**.

If the Rockies are playing at home and you know they're going to be ridiculously popular, you have three broad options:

1) Play the chalk—the Rockies—since they're the highest-projected team.

2) Go completely contrarian with a team like the Padres that few users will have.

3) Use a mix, balancing usage with expected production to field a high-upside team that's still antifragile.

If you side with Option 1, you'll maximize your points over the long run. BUT, if Colorado has a big game, you might still be competing with, say, 30 percent of the field who also rostered the Rockies. That's a big problem.

If you go with Option 2, you'll be locked and loaded if the Padres go nuts. But the odds of that are so slim that it's probably not even worth it. I'd rather have 10 percent equity in a $100 million company than 50% equity in a company that isn't worth shit.

If you balance those two strategies, though, you can potentially find enough value to make going semi-contrarian worth it. You'll have a decent opportunity for your stack to pay off with a big game, and more important, you'll be in the best possible position to actually benefit from that since you won't need to compete with as many other DraftKings users.

A key component in my view is understanding that there's likely to be a whole lot of overlap within the top decile of ownership; we all know that Colorado is a high-value play pretty much every time they're at Coors Field. On the other hand, the second and third deciles of ownership are often much more mixed. My hypothesis is that that's where we want to be, combining relatively high value with relatively low usage.

Ultimately, this all comes down to the data. **We'd of course expect the lineups in the top decile of ownership to win the most since they're using the most high-value players—and that's what we see—but from a practical standpoint, there could be more usable value in sliding down in ownership just a bit to avoid the lineup overlap that I think will ultimately maximize your projected points, but hurt your win probability**.

So how can we test for this? My idea was to look at the average number of points needed to win GPPs for lineups in each ownership decile. The idea is that the "sweet spot" should be where users are winning with the lowest scores—a direct reflection of an antifragile approach to daily fantasy baseball.

Remember, we want to benefit from chaos, i.e. other users making wrong predictions. When the crowd is wrong, scores will be down. And when overall scores are down, we want to position ourselves to gain the most. So here's a look at the average score needed to win large-slate GPPs—those with at least 10 MLB games—based on ownership deciles. The first decile, for example, is made up of the top 10 percent of all lineups in a tournament in terms of cumulative ownership, aka the chalk.

Decile of Cumulative Ownership	Avg Cumulative Ownership	% of GPPs Won	Avg Score of Winning Entry
1st	342%	25.9%	167.6
2nd	251%	12.0%	158.9
3rd	212%	10.0%	158.9
4th	185%	9.4%	157.2
5th	163%	9.2%	158.2
6th	144%	6.3%	156.2
7th	126%	7.2%	157.3
8th	109%	7.5%	158.8
9th	90%	7.8%	160.2
10th	62%	4.7%	169.1

Bingo. **Even though the high-usage lineups in the first decile have understandably won the highest rate of tournaments, they've also "needed" to score 167.6 points to do so. That's a high number—much higher than the score needed to win in all except the last decile**.

Another way to look at it is this: **when you play the chalk, you're "forcing" yourself to be really good since, if you're right, you still need to compete with so many users and ultimately hit on all or most of your plays. When you're contrarian, you're basically giving yourself "outs" so that you don't need to be nearly as sharp**.

The fact that lineups in the second through ninth ownership deciles have won with an average score that's significantly less than that needed to win with a "chalk" lineup in the top decile of ownership suggests that this is a sort of "sweet

spot" for balancing usage and value; you always want to roster players and teams that are underpriced and have lots of upside, sure, but the smartest tactic might be jumping down a peg from the "obvious" play of the day—using a "best-of-the-rest" strategy, so to speak.

Okay, now let's compare large slates to medium-sizes slates with between five and nine games.

Decile of Cumulative Ownership	Avg Cumulative Ownership	% of GPPs Won	Avg Score of Winning Entry
1st	413%	22.3%	163.2
2nd	302%	9.9%	154.5
3rd	256%	10.1%	150.6
4th	227%	8.2%	151.8
5th	204%	8.4%	154.4
6th	183%	7.0%	158.1
7th	164%	8.8%	157.9
8th	144%	10.1%	161.3
9th	123%	9.5%	154.8
10th	91%	5.8%	160.1

Basically the same sort of deal. And how about short slates?

Decile of Cumulative Ownership	Avg Cumulative Ownership	% of GPPs Won	Avg Score of Winning Entry
1st	578%	24.9%	139.0
2nd	469%	9.3%	132.4
3rd	419%	9.4%	130.3
4th	376%	9.7%	135.0
5th	341%	9.0%	131.8
6th	311%	9.1%	133.3
7th	282%	10.2%	136.8
8th	252%	9.1%	140.0
9th	218%	5.2%	145.2
10th	166%	3.9%	137.2

Again, a similar effect. Remember, there are two keys to understanding why this data suggests you should be at least semi-contrarian: the fact that there's a lot of overlap in the top decile of ownership and the notion that we're not trying to maximize points scored, but rather maximize win probability. We'd naturally expect the top decile of lineups (in terms of ownership) to win the most GPPs, and by a wide margin, because those are the highest-value teams. But there's a difference between that idea versus us individually maximizing the probability of our single lineup winning.

There's more proof of that in the fact that the low-ownership deciles require a high score to win. Those lineups have really low-usage players—completely contrarian, but also super low-value—so they're forced to score way more points than the contrarian-but-not-totally-fucking-crazy lineups.

I'm going to have some individual team data in the appendix of this book that will help demonstrate this concept even more, but here's a sneak peek...

Team Stacked	Avg Points	% GPPs Won	% of LUs which Won
Colorado	107.5	5.4%	0.38%
Los Angeles	104.0	2.7%	0.26%
Miami	103.3	1.5%	0.28%
Baltimore	100.0	3.0%	0.27%
Washington	100.0	2.1%	0.23%
Atlanta	99.4	1.4%	0.19%
Cleveland	99.0	2.0%	0.16%
Arizona	98.6	1.5%	0.28%
Milwaukee	98.1	4.0%	0.40%
Pittsburgh	97.4	2.2%	0.20%

In 2014, the Rockies led to the most GPP tournament victories at 5.4 percent. However, they weren't the MVP of stacks, so to speak, because **the chances of you using a Rockies stack and winning—a much different idea than any of the many Colorado stacks winning a GPP—was actually less than if you rostered the Brewers (due to reduced ownership). On top of that, Milwaukee lineups averaged 9.4 fewer points than Colorado lineups last season, yet were still the Most Valuable Stack.**

There's somewhat of a correlation between overall GPPs won and each lineup's chances of winning, but it's weak. In looking at the worst stacks of 2014 in terms of points scored (not pictured), you'd see that **Philadelphia lineups—an offense that led to the *fewest fantasy points* of any team—actually had a 0.27 percent chance of winning a GPP—greater than the Dodgers, who scored the *second-most* points!**

I charted the average winning score for MLB GPPs based on ownership and slate size just to help you visualize what's going on.

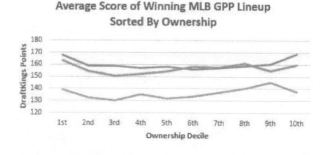

There are small variations, but the general idea stands across each slate size: **if you're going to go with the chalk, you're**

going to need to score more points than if you drop down just a bit in ownership. After the moderate ownership lineups, though, the average winning score creeps back up due to super-low-ownership players also being poor plays; there's a reason no one wants them, and we're simply trying to find a nice balance between rostering quality players and minimizing how well they must perform to actually benefit.

So should you be a contrarian in daily fantasy baseball tournaments? Well, yes and no. You probably don't want to go off of the reservation with your pitchers (does that mean to use pitchers from the Indians?), but you also don't need to get too crazy with your batter selections either; it's not like it's the ridiculously contrarian, off-the-wall lineups that are having success, but rather simply those that fade the obvious play in favor of moderately owned players with high ceilings.

The take-home point: **Consider skipping the obvious stacks— perhaps the Cubs with the wind blowing out at Wrigley or Toronto at home—and instead side with high-upside offenses that won't see top-tier player utilization.**

And just for fun, here's a look at the average player usage in each decile...

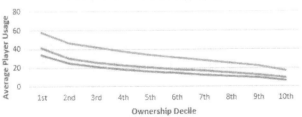

I don't think this is terribly actionable information—more just interesting—but it does lend credence to the idea that there's more overlap in the top decile of ownership than elsewhere; the drop in average player utilization from the first decile to the second, even in terms of percentages, is much larger than from any other decile to another.

6. You should maximize expected points in cash games: FALSE

We've already seen that trying to maximize your expected points in tournaments necessarily means following the herd, which is typically a poor strategy in most situations. And while I think it makes sense to play the top values in cash games—regardless of anticipated usage—that doesn't mean you should always be looking to maximize your median projection.

I'm specifically considering pitching and the merits of "overpaying" for elite arms. Because pitching is so consistent, it makes sense to narrow the range of potential outcomes in cash games by "buying insurance" on top pitchers. The pure dollar-per-point values might not be there, but you can significantly enhance your lineup's floor by allocating a high percentage of your cap to pitching. That will likely reduce your long-term projected points, but increase your win probability.

Imagine a completely extreme example in which you can choose between two strategies, one of which always results in 110 points, and the other of which leads to a 50 percent chance of 70 points and a 50 percent chance of 170 points.

In terms of expected points, the latter scenario is superior because you'll average 120 points. If you utilize that strategy in GPPs, you'll crush it because you'll win a whole shitload of tournaments scoring 170 points. However, employ that *exact same strategy* in 50/50s and you'll be a losing player, winning just half of all leagues.

This is clearly a hypothetical, but it illustrates the idea that **what matters isn't simply expected points, but also the anticipated distribution of scores.**

But How Many Points Do I Need?

Before moving on to batter selection strategy, let's take a look at the average scores needed to win different league types on DraftKings.

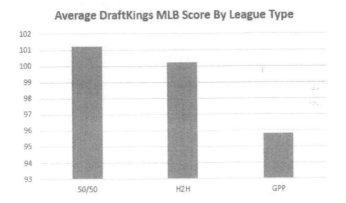

In terms of pure points, **50/50s are the toughest leagues with an average MLB score of 101.2, which is just a tad higher than the average head-to-head score of 100.2**. Meanwhile, take a look at GPPs; **with an average score of only 95.8, tournaments as a whole appear to be far weaker than cash games.**

I think there are a couple reasons for this. One is that users don't care about safety in tournaments and are far more likely to take a flier on a player who might not be the best value. As I've shown, I don't think that's necessarily a poor strategy—it depends on how you pull it off—but it certainly drags down the average GPP score.

The second reason GPP scores are so low is that there are simply worse players. Although cash games can be your most consistent source of daily fantasy profits, tournaments are weaker, in my opinion, because they attract every type of player. Most newbies who come onto DraftKings want to spend a little to make a lot. **You need to be careful with putting too much of your bankroll into GPPs on a day-to-day basis because there's a ton of variance—you can run cold for a long time due to nothing but poor luck—but I definitely believe tournaments offer the best ROI if they're approached optimally.**

Another way to face worse competition is of course to play at lower stakes. Although there can be quality players at low stakes (and shitty players at high stakes), there's a correlation between the average MLB score and the buy-in level.

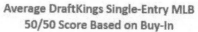

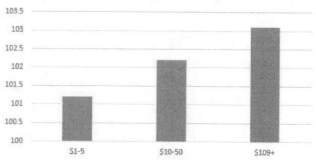

Average DraftKings Single-Entry MLB 50/50 Score Based on Buy-In

The average single-entry 50/50 score in small-stakes games of $1 to $5 is 101.2. That jumps one point to 102.2 in $10-$50 games, and nearly another full point to 103.1 in games with a buy-in amount of at least $109.

This shouldn't be particularly surprising, but it's certainly evidence that small changes in overall numbers or percentages can mean a lot when you're talking about a sample size of leagues as large as what we're dealing with. We know that high-stakes games will naturally have superior players, so the fact that the difference between those guys and the small-stakes players is just a couple points suggests that other seemingly minor deviations that we've seen—such as the 0.5 percentage point difference in salary cap allocation for pitchers in cashing versus non-cashing lineups—are meaningful.

And in case you're curious, there is a difference in scoring in single-entry versus multi-entry 50/50s, but perhaps not in the direction you'd assume; **in low-stakes games, the average multi-entry 50/50 score is only 99.8—1.4 points behind single-entry 50/50 games at the same stakes**. It could be the case that the casual player is drawn to multi-entry 50/50s more so than single-entry leagues, bringing down the average score needed to cash.

CSURAM88's Analysis

As I mentioned in the last chapter, I'm a big cash-game player, so I'm most concerned with creating a high floor for my lineup. My strategy in cash games is much different than in tournaments, where I'm obviously more risk-seeking and try to increase the ceiling of my lineup as much as possible.

Although baseball is volatile from night to night, there are still certain player types who are more consistent than others. Pitchers who typically throw a lot of innings, for example, have pretty high floors, even if they aren't strikeout monsters. Starting someone like Danny Salazar can be very risky in cash games, even if he offers value, because he's a high-variance option; he might strike out 10 batters, but he could also get pulled after the third inning. The same thing goes for a batter like Adam Dunn. I emphasize rostering players who will provide me predictable production, for the most part. That usually means avoiding "blow-up pitchers" and hitters who strike out a lot.

When it comes to cash games, one of the things that's really important to me is maximizing plate appearances. When you start using players who hit at the bottom of the order, their production will naturally be more volatile because they're likely to see fewer at-bats than their teammates. That's a really important factor to me—just getting as much exposure as I can to as many plate appearances as possible.

In tournaments, there's a lot of merit to fading high-usage players or teams in baseball. Whereas I'm almost strictly value-based in basketball, even in GPPs, baseball is a totally different game. It's event-based and difficult to predict, which means it can make a lot of sense to be contrarian if you know a particular player is going to have high ownership.

> *"A ship is safest in the harbor, but that's not what ships are for."*
>
> *William G.T. Shedd*

IV. Chasing Dongs: Selecting Batters in Daily Fantasy Baseball

> *"I have stressed this distinction because it is an important one. It defines the fundamental difference between probability and statistics: the former concerns predictions based on fixed probabilities; the latter concerns the inference of those probabilities based on observed data."*
>
> Leonard Mlodinow

1st

1st

1st

That's the Oakland Athletics' rank in fly ball rate over the past three seasons. To give some context to just how much of an outlier the A's have been, consider that the difference between their 2014 fly ball rate and that of the second-place team in fly ball rate—the Cubs—was greater than that between the Cubs and the next 19 teams in Major League Baseball.

Um, think they've found something they like?

Known for their Moneyball-driven decision-making over the years, the A's are consistently among the most innovative teams in baseball. They search for every little edge they can get, exploiting inefficiencies in the free agent market by identifying predictors of success that haven't been factored into a player's perceived worth.

And that's exactly what we're trying to do, too: search for players whose actual worth exceeds their cost (i.e. their DraftKings salary). To uncover that value, though, we can't use traditional bulk stats like batting average or home runs. If we're looking for a home run hitter who has gone deep five times in the past six games, we're probably very unlikely to generate value since his expected production is likely already priced into his salary. If we can find some bats that haven't gone deep but are showing signs that they might—maybe favorable ISO splits, strong gusts of wind to center, or an advantageous GB/FB ratio—then we can beat the market to fit as much potential upside into our lineups for as cheaply as possible.

Again, my method for sifting through batters is typically a top-down one; I start by analyzing which offenses could produce big-time numbers in a specific game, considering the Vegas lines, weather, ballpark, batting order, and so on. Such an approach makes sense when you consider the strong correlation between teammates' fantasy production.

In addition to analyzing offensive splits, I consider pitcher splits, too. In that way, hitter and pitcher research is very closely linked, and I think a lot of daily fantasy players overlook this relationship. They might see that CC Sabathia has one of the highest K/9 numbers against left-handed batters over the past three years (11.89), yet they don't examine how the opponent performs against southpaws. If it's an offense that crushes left-handed pitching, Sabathia's matchup might actually be a neutral one when it initially appears very favorable.

With that said, I've already outlined a lot of the stats and characteristics I look for when selecting my batters. This chapter is going to take a more in-depth look at those items and some other aspects of my daily fantasy baseball hitter selection.

Maximizing Home Run Probability

I've talked a lot about the importance of home runs and why we should be searching for them in many occasions—even in cash games. In a nutshell, the reward for home runs exceeds the risk in paying for them, particularly because home run rate is a good proxy for overall power and fantasy production; it's not like guys who go deep are incapable of scoring fantasy points in other ways.

Let me rephrase that. It's not like guys NOT NAMED ADAM DUNN who go deep are incapable of scoring fantasy points in other ways.

So while I don't emphasize power and home run probability at all costs, it's certainly a major factor in my analysis. Here are some of the ways I go about gettin' all dem dingers.

Lefty/Righty Splits and Home Runs

There are all sorts of ways to analyze lefty/righty splits. Even casual fans understand that hitters usually perform worse against pitchers of the same "handedness," but few realize the effect is different for lefties and righties.

If you recall, there are pretty big splits in OPS based on handedness for both lefties and righties.

OPS Splits Since 2000 (Top 150 Hitters)			
	LHP	RHP	Difference
LHB	0.738	0.846	0.108
RHB	0.894	0.811	0.083

And the differences are magnified for left-handed bats, who struggle against southpaws way more than right-handed batters have trouble versus right-handed arms.

Baseball is such a binary sport—a player either hits a home run or doesn't, for example—so it isn't surprising to see that somewhat small differences in OPS turn into a major difference in home run rates.

	At-Bats/HR Splits Since 2000 (Top 150 Hitters)		
	LHP	RHP	Difference
LHB	32.2	22.2	10
RHB	20.5	22.7	2.2

In terms of raw power, left-handed batters don't go deep as often as right-handed batters. That's not really actionable information because we only need to be concerned about an individual hitter's chances of going deep in any given game, and the overall rate for other batters of his handedness isn't going to tell us much.

However, it's definitely useful to know how lefties and righties generally perform in certain situations because those effects tend to carry over from hitter to hitter, and the top-hitting lefties have taken southpaws deep once every 32.2 at-bats since 2000, which is way worse than every other batter/pitcher split. Right-handed bats are worse against right-handed pitching, but the effect isn't nearly as great as lefty-on-lefty; actually, **right-handed batters have been nearly equally likely to take a righty deep as they are to hit a home run against a left-handed pitcher**.

The difference on the right side of the chart is what I care about most, as it shows that **left-handed hitters are far more pitcher-dependent for their production (or at least their power) than right-handed bats. Overall, there's no worse**

situation than to trot a left-handed hitter out there against a southpaw.

For more evidence of this effect, check out these 2014 ISO heat maps, courtesy of FanGraphs. The first is how righties hit off of right-handed pitching.

All MLB Batters ISO/P vs R as R
Season: 2010 to 2014 | Count: All | Total Pitches: 1278390 | Viewpoint: Batter

The highest ISO/P numbers unsurprisingly occurred over the middle and inner portions of the plate, and they're as high as 0.089. Meanwhile, here's the lefty vs. lefty heat map.

All MLB Batters ISO/P vs L as L
Season: 2010 to 2014 | Count: All | Total Pitches: 297404 | Viewpoint: Batter

The highest total is just 0.078. Simply put, lefties struggle against lefty pitchers way, way more than righties versus right-handed arms.

If you're analyzing an individual player in a single matchup, his career splits are going to be more valuable than overall numbers. Some lefty bats don't struggle as much versus lefty arms as others. I think it makes sense to consider aggregate numbers when you don't have a sufficient sample size of data (such as with a rookie or second-year player), but generally individual splits trump overall splits (though the two often resemble one another).

In tournaments, though, a popular daily fantasy baseball strategy is to stack players on the same team—the 2-3-4-5 hitters on a single offense, for example—in which case I think it makes sense to consider the overall rates. You're not going to find an entire offense of left-handed hitters who collectively hit well against left-handed pitchers, for example.

If there's one actionable item to take from this data, I think it's that **you can run primarily right-handed stacks out there against both lefty and righty pitchers**, **but you need to be more careful with lefty hitters**, who can be in a really poor spot against not only lefty starters, but also lefty relief.

Of course, the flip side of that argument is that lefties are much better against right-handed pitching. If DraftKings players are typically priced according to their overall numbers (which is probably the case), then **lefty bats against right-handed pitching will offer more value than righties versus lefty arms (because of the larger deviation in splits for lefty batters)**.

That means that rolling out a primarily left-handed stack against a right-handed pitcher might offer both value and upside, which is ideal in any tournament. Of course, it's still a risk given that a left-handed stack will often face left-handed relief, which could result in 1) poor matchups for your hitters late in the game or 2) even worse, your hitters getting pinch-hit for with a righty bat.

Looking at this data and thinking about how managers work in the final few innings of baseball games, I think it's safe to say that right-handed batters are far less volatile than lefties since their power isn't so reliant on a specific handedness of pitcher. And since much of winning a tournament is about maximizing the overall probability of your bats realizing their upside, you could make an argument that righty-dominant stacks as a whole trump left-handed stacks.

Home Runs vs Batted Ball Profiles

I'm always trying to steal valuable intel—being a thief is, like, the most vital part of being a profitable daily fantasy sports player, right?—so I definitely became very interested in fly ball rates, battled ball profiles, and GB/FB ratios once I noticed the A's have been emphasizing the same.

So I looked into this stuff, and I have some pretty cool data. First, here's a look at the True Average (batting average adjusted for park effects, among other things) in nine possible batter/pitcher matchups.

	FB Pitcher	Neutral Pitcher	GB Pitcher
FB Batter	0.271	0.276	0.275
Neutral Batter	0.270	0.267	0.258
GB Batter	0.240	0.229	0.221

Data provided by regressing.deadspin.com

The first thing that jumps out is that batters who are considered "ground ball hitters"—those who hit a ground ball in at least half of their at-bats—are pretty shitty as a whole. Ground ball hitters match up best against fly ball pitchers, yet they have still posted only a .240 TAv against them.

Meanwhile, **fly ball hitters are the best of the bunch, including the only type of batters that don't struggle (and actually excel) versus ground ball pitchers**. Fly ball hitters can face any pitcher type and have success, while ground ball batters are far superior against fly ball pitchers than anyone else.

There's been a recent shift among MLB teams to more and more ground ball pitchers, and Oakland has tried to exploit that trend by securing as many hitters as possible who can take advantage of those arms; when batters who tend to hit the ball in the air match up with pitchers who tend to induce ground balls, the result is often a positive one for the hitter.

Here's a look at slugging percentage versus GB/FB ratio. . .

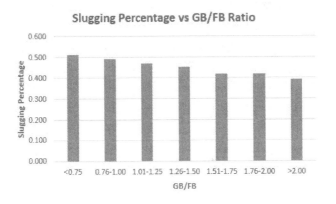

There's a very linear relationship, with higher ground ball rates leading to less and less power. That makes sense, obviously, since you generally need to get the ball into the air to hit for extra bases. It's worth noting that GB/FB ratio is one of the most consistent stat out there for pitchers, too, with a 0.75 strength of correlation from year to year—more consistent than a pitcher's K/9.

That means that **we can predict ground ball and fly ball rates with really quality accuracy; the same bats tend to hit the ball into the air and the same arms tend to allow the ball to be hit into the air.**

And if we look at the average number of home runs broken down by GB/FB ratio, we see that it's the hitters who can avoid ground balls who continually offer the most power, and thus the most access to home runs and, ultimately, fantasy production.

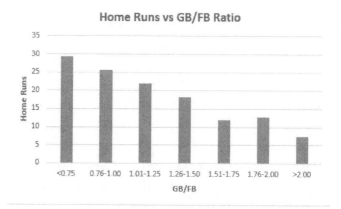

And here's a look at the average number of at-bats per home run allowed since 2000 for the three categories of pitchers...

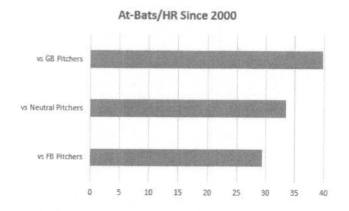

Fly ball pitchers allow a batter to go deep around 25 percent more often than ground ball pitchers. If you're continually giving yourself exposure to batters with favorable splits in terms of both handedness and batted ball profiles, you can significantly enhance your probability of squeezing home runs out of your lineup.

Now throw in information on the Vegas lines, weather, and park factors, and you can see how some daily fantasy players field lineups that have a whole lot more upside than others.

I offer info on splits and batted ball profiles in my Daily Fantasy Baseball Package at FantasyFootballDrafting.com.

Stolen Bases

Though I generally target players who have the ability to go deep, I will forfeit that in the case of base-stealers. I still emphasize power over speed, for a couple reasons. One is that stolen bases are even more challenging to predict. The second is that **steals don't "lead" to any other fantasy production; the ability to hit home runs results in power numbers in other areas, whereas the ability to swipe bags isn't necessarily a useful proxy for other fantasy stats**.

In any event, I think **most of predicting stolen bases is just about finding players who are likely to get on base**. That means hitting near the top of the order and of course being in a favorable matchup. **Even for base-stealers, I care more about their matchup with the pitcher than their likelihood of stealing a bag once they're on**.

A lot of daily fantasy players care about the handedness of the pitcher when projecting steals since lefties are obviously in a better position to hold a runner on first base. Here's a look at stolen base rates since 2000, broken down by pitcher handedness.

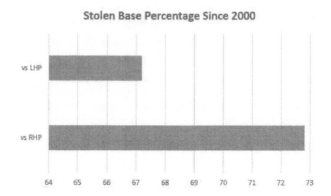

Against lefties, base-stealers are caught less than one-third of the time. Against righties, it's around 27 percent of the time. That's a small difference—meaningful, but probably not enough to avoid base-stealers versus lefties.

Now take a look at the number of steals per plate appearance. I researched this data to adjust for batters simply not taking off against lefty arms.

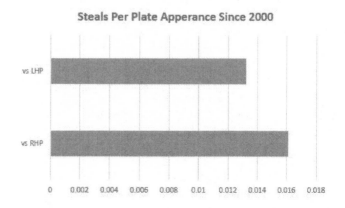

We're looking at 0.016 steals per plate appearance against right-handed pitching and 0.013 steals per plate appearance versus lefties—a difference of around 19 percent. That's enough to conclude that, while you don't need to avoid base-stealers against left-handed pitching, it's certainly advantageous to get them against righties.

Of course, the catcher matters, too. In 2014, the top qualifying catcher threw runners out 37.2 percent of the time, while the worst catcher checked in at just 16.7 percent. One thing to keep in mind is that the percentage of runners a catcher throws out can fluctuate pretty wildly from year to year, negating the large deviation between catchers for the most part. **There are certain arms that are always near the top—Yadier Molina and Miguel Montero come to mind— and those are the catchers I avoid when targeting base-stealers.** Other than those arms, I'd say I'm not as concerned about the base-stealing matchup as others; instead, I just want exposure to speedsters who are going to first find a way to get on base.

Batting Order

In the research chapter, I posted this graph displaying how plate appearances and fantasy production are distributed.

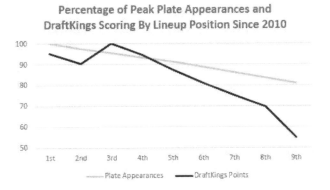

Percentage of Peak Plate Appearances and DraftKings Scoring By Lineup Position Since 2010

Leadoff hitters necessarily obtain the most plate appearances, but they've historically produced the second-most fantasy points on DraftKings (behind No. 3 hitters). You can see that there's historically been drop-off in fantasy production around the No. 6 hitter.

Now let's compare that data with historical win rates from DraftKings.

Latest Batter in Lineup	% of Lineups Cashing 50/50s	% of Lineups Cashing GPPs
4th	52.3%	19.4%
5th	52.3%	21.1%
6th	51.8%	21.2%
7th	49.9%	21.0%
8th	49.0%	20.6%
9th	48.8%	20.7%

Very interesting. There's a very linear relationship when it comes to 50/50 success and the slots in which your batters hit. Specifically, **the safe play seems to be acquire as many plate appearances as possible**. Here's a look at how 50/50 win rates change based on the batting order.

Pretty clear trend, with an obvious drop around the seventh spot in the order. **If you're looking for consistency, it's probably in your best interest to use as many bats at the top of the order as possible. In rostering hitters at the bottom of the order, you're unnecessarily reducing plate appearances**.

Now let's compare that data to the win rate in GPPs.

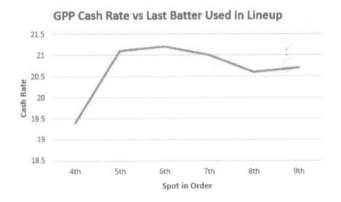

The exact opposite. **In tournaments, using hitters early in the order could unnecessarily limit your upside**. It's usually the 3-6 hitters who possess the most power. It appears the extra plate appearances you can acquire by using bats at the top of the order isn't enough to make up for the reduced ceiling.

Also note that part of this effect is probably due to stacking. You could potentially stack 1-2-3-4 hitters from a single team, sure, but most stacks use at least one bat that's farther down in the order.

Finally, note that **the rate of cashing in GPPs doesn't fall off much with the use of 7-8-9 hitters**. I think this is probably due to those bats being low-usage players. Hitters used late in the order usually don't offer a ton of upside and they limit your ceiling on plate appearances, but they're also rarely utilized by daily fantasy players. I think **an underrated tournament strategy is to play a chalk offense, like the Rockies at home, but roster players late in the order who would see reduced ownership**.

Either way, this is really interesting data that suggests you should maximize plate appearances to increase safety, but perhaps forgo early-in-the-order bats to increase upside and reduce usage in GPPs.

Salary Cap Allocation

Salary cap allocation is a really interesting topic in daily fantasy sports, but one that's really challenging to transform into actionable information. The reason is that each day is so unique that it can be difficult to apply very broad numbers about what works (in certain situations).

However, I still think there's some value in salary cap allocation data, for a couple reasons. The first is that, as I've mentioned, **the amount of randomness in baseball means we should side with long-term trends and data more so than in any other sport**; we just aren't as good at predicting the future as we think.

The second reason is that **it's valuable to analyze past lineups (once you've built up a large enough sample size) to see if you have any biases in your roster construction**. If you study two months of MLB data and find that you're paying $800 less on pitchers than the average winning lineup, that's a pretty huge deal. Aggregate salary cap allocation data can help you understand if you're on the right track.

We've already seen that lineups that paid more for pitching performed better last season, in both cash games and GPPs. And though there are certainly times I'll take a flier on a high-upside pitcher with lots of strikeout potential, I generally like to save some money on my bats, too.

But what sort of batter salary cap allocation method has worked best in the past: a high/low strategy or a balanced one? For the purposes of this data, I defined a high/low strategy as one with four or more batters below one standard deviation of the mean salary at their position.

Strategy	50/50 % Cashed	GPP % Cashed
High/Low	51.8%	21.7%
Balanced	48.5%	19.6%

In both cash games and GPPs, high/low strategies have been the most successful. I don't think this is evidence that you should punt multiple positions in order to afford top-priced bats and create a "stars and scrubs" lineup, but I do think it points to the significance of hitting on cheap values. It doesn't take much production for him to return value, and he also comes with the added benefit of salary cap relief.

Punt Plays

The key to succeeding with high/low roster construction is of course identifying high-value punt plays. Here's a look at how punt plays have historically performed at each position on DraftKings.

Position	Max Punt Salary	Avg Fantasy Points
1B	$3,800	7.32
2B	$3,100	6.18
3B	$3,400	6.37
SS	$3,000	5.88
OF	$3,500	7.23
C	$3,000	6.58

To be considered a punt, a batter needed to be in at least 10 percent of lineups and priced at least one standard deviation below the mean at his position. I also charted the number of points you could expect per dollar spent on punt plays.

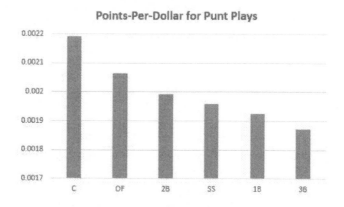

Points-Per-Dollar for Punt Plays

Even though I don't use dollar-per-point or points-per-dollar (they're two versions of the same thing) on a daily basis in baseball, I think it's fine to analyze aggregate data in this way because we're dealing with such large numbers—every punt play over the course of an entire season. Further, it isn't like these value calculations are "wrong," per se, but rather that we shouldn't use them to select individual players. Over the long run, though, it's of course beneficial to consistently get exposure to the highest-value players.

You might argue that we need to know the overall points-per-dollar at each respective position before drawing conclusions. No. 1: Don't shoot the messenger. No. 2: NO WE DON'T. Well I don't think so, anyway, because remember that each position has a different price point for what constitutes a "punt" play, and that price is dictated by the overall salary distribution on DraftKings, which is of course linked to anticipated player production, i.e. expected positional production is a component of the punt play salary figures.

In any event, you can make of this information what you'd like. I don't think there's anything terribly actionable here—the data is probably just due to variance—and every day offers unique options. Understanding when to punt and the merits of the strategy in general, however, is important.

Batter Scoring Based on Salary and Ownership

One of the important aspects of punting a position is understanding how players are expected to perform in certain salary tiers. If you can match that up with ownership rates, it can really aid in your GPP play.

Here's a really cool look at 2014 fantasy scoring for batters, broken down by their ownership and salaries.

		Percentile of Salary				
		Top 20%	Second 20%	Middle 20%	Fourth 20%	Bottom 20%
Percentile of Ownership	Top 20%	13.0	8.3	7.7	7.0	6.1
	Second 20%	10.5	7.4	7.2	6.4	6.1
	Middle 20%	9.9	7.2	6.5	6.2	5.8
	Fourth 20%	9.0	6.3	6.1	5.3	5.1
	Bottom 20%	7.6	4.5	3.9	3.5	2.3

There's a whole lot of interesting stuff going on here. First, I think there's some useful information regarding when it's smart to go against the grain and/or fade players who you expect to be high-usage.

To quantify the relationship between usage and salary, I charted the average fantasy production for each of the 10 buckets—the five ownership buckets and the five salary buckets.

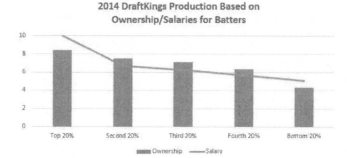

2014 DraftKings Production Based on Ownership/Salaries for Batters

Historically, the top 20 percent of batters in terms of price have performed better than the top 20 percent in terms of usage (which includes players from all salary levels). The only other bucket in which that phenomenon occurs is the bottom 20 percent, where the cheapest players have outperformed the least popular.

Another way to interpret the data is in terms of scarcity. "I'm thinking of going against the grain in one of a few different spots. Which salary level is the riskiest in terms of trying to reproduce that production?"

To determine that, I calculated the difference between expected production for players in the top 20 percent in ownership versus those in the second 20 percent. Basically, we're looking at the difference between "chalk" plays versus "valuable-but-not-obvious" plays. Here's that difference, sorted into the five salary buckets.

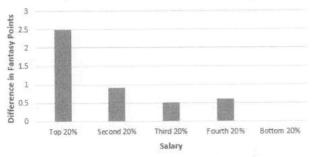

Historically, it has been the most dangerous to fade the chalk in the top tier of pricing, i.e. when a top-priced player is an obvious value, you should probably play him. This fits with my suggested salary cap allocation of generally paying up for pitchers and individual value bats while saving money on your offensive stack.

One of the potential problems is that we don't know player usage before leagues begin. That's certainly an issue, but the overarching idea is that it's risky to fade top-priced players when they're also obvious values.

Also note that it doesn't appear to be risky at all to fade the popular punt plays of the day. Yes, that $3000 second basemen getting a spot start might be the "obvious" value, but since such players don't have a ton of upside anyway, even if they're clear values, they also don't possess much scarcity; there's not a massive opportunity cost associated with missing on an obvious punt play, but there's a huge potential cost in missing out on Trout or Cabrera or Donaldson when they go 4-for-5 with three dongs.

Benefiting from Randomness

Though every day is unique, we now have some general heuristics for batter selection. Here's another one that you can add to that list: **Buy low on underachieving players**.

In the intro, I mentioned that I often find myself jumping on players whose price has recently fallen—both batters and pitchers—due to poor recent play. It's not that I think that some form of streaky play is impossible—whether it's due to changes in confidence, health, or whatever, I think players' anticipated "mean" production shifts due to a variety of factors—but that doesn't mean we can use that information in any predictive way.

It's really, really easy to get fooled by randomness in baseball. Is that player who is 9-for-12 in his last three games really "hot?" The answer is I have no fucking clue—I don't think I can separate a signal from the noise in a very high percentage of situations—so I'd prefer to pay as cheap of a price as possible given the inability to make accurate predictions.

Hot and cold streaks are a vague sort of thing very similar to "momentum" in the NFL—there until it's gone and gone until it's there. But I do think we can and should make an attempt to quantify short-term fluctuations in randomness. If we can do that, we'll have a better idea if a player has been lucky or not—if he's hitting a ton of home runs because he's really crushing the ball or if he's just gotten lucky with placement, for example.

BABIP

BABIP—Batting Average on Balls in Play—is a player's batting average...on balls...that he hits into play. Shocker.

There are a few factors that can cause BABIP to fluctuate—talent level and defense among them—but the most important factor in determining a player's BABIP is just luck. **BABIP is a decent proxy for the luck a player has experienced because it can capture how often those cheap bloopers have fallen in for hits or how frequently hard-hit line drives have been straight at a defender**.

Again, not every player's long-term BABIP will be the same, but most players' BABIP regresses toward .300. When a hitter's BABIP is well below .300, it means that he's probably been unlucky with batted ball placement—something that's extremely difficult to control—and will probably see an improvement in overall numbers in the future.

Thus, for our purposes, a high BABIP is a bad thing, suggesting a decline in numbers in the near future. In general, it makes sense to target sluggers that we know can mash but just have a low BABIP, particularly to start a season. Once that variance levels out, they'll post superior fantasy stats, even if they aren't actually performing any better on the field.

HR/FB

HR/FB—home runs per fly ball—is similar to BABIP in that we'd expect players to have different numbers, even over the long run, but the short-term numbers are difficult to separate from randomness. That means **we can use HR/FB, in conjunction with other numbers, to help determine how much of a player's home run total is due to variance**.

I like to compare a player's HR/FB ratio in a given season to his personal average from the prior year or two. That way, we can adjust for his power level (to an extent), to help capture how lucky he's been.

For the average player, around 9-10 percent of fly balls result in home runs. But again, it differs based on the player. Whenever a batter has hit a home run on more than 20 percent of his fly balls for any significant period of time, though, we can expect some sort of regression moving forward.

Predictive Over Explanatory

There are a number of similar stats I like to use—Weighted Runs Created, Batted Ball Profiles, Plate Discipline, and so on—but the concept behind them is always the same: make accurate predictions. There are lots of interesting stats that can effectively explain past events, but not predict future ones.

In football, a team's run/pass balance is one such stat. In general, running the ball is associated with winning. How many times have you heard "Team X has won Y straight games when running back Z gets 25 carries?" The problem is that run plays explain the past, but don't help us predict the future; teams run *because* they're already winning, not the other way around, and being bullish on truly run-heavy teams, as a rule, probably isn't that smart.

Similarly, a batter's average or home run total will help us determine how effective he's been in the past, but they aren't the most effective tools we can use to predict his future performance.

Ultimately, emphasizing the predictive over the explanatory reduces our risk. If you're bullish on a hitter who is rolling—say, four straight games with a dong—you're typically going to be overpaying for him in a worst-case scenario and getting what you pay for (long-term) in a best-case scenario. Bulk stats like home runs are priced into DraftKings salaries.

Meanwhile, if you buy low on a struggling player who has shown signs of improved play—a hitter who has been on the wrong side of variance—then you're getting what you pay for as a worst-case scenario and finding sensational value in a best-case scenario.

If beating the daily fantasy baseball market is about maximizing the difference between anticipated production and price, then it will always make sense to emphasize predictive stats (a component of anticipated production) over explanatory stats (a major factor in determining price).

CSURAM88's Analysis

I already laid out a bit of my strategy when selecting hitters; I consider the Vegas lines a lot, especially projected runs for certain offenses, as well as wOBA and ISO. Everything is broken down by handedness. I almost never use a batter unless he has favorable splits against a particular handedness of pitcher.

Park factors are also a big component of my batter selection. When hitters who play their home games in a pitcher's park travel somewhere like Coors Field, it's an absolutely massive advantage for them. And vice versa; when a team like the Rockies travels to a less hitter-friendly park, they need to be downgraded.

I also think people don't consider stolen base upside enough in their hitters. I like to target base-stealers against the league's worst catchers when it comes to throwing guys out. Stolen bases aren't extremely predictable from game to game, but you'll get them if you keep giving yourself chances.

Also, sites like DraftKings will often force you to pay a premium for power hitters, whereas base-stealers can come more cheaply.

As far as BvP is concerned, it's not something I consider. There's way too much noise in those results for it to be useful. I do look at recent performance, though, and I target batters who actually aren't performing well of late. People are so quick to react to a player's recent performance, so when a hitter's price drops because he has only one hit in his last four games, for example, he's typically going to offer value. We can't tell much about how a hitter is going to perform in a specific matchup by looking at his last few games.

"Nature almost surely operates by combining chance with necessity, randomness with determinism."

- Eric Chaisson

V. An Arms Race: Selecting Pitchers in Daily Fantasy Baseball

"Engage people with what they expect; it is what they are able to discern and confirms their projections. It settles them into predictable patterns of response, occupying their minds while you wait for the extraordinary moment—that which they cannot anticipate."

Sun Tzu

Warren Buffett once said, "Be fearful when others are greedy and greedy when others are fearful." I think that's pretty sound advice for pretty much all aspects of life, but especially the most important one—DFS.

Neither risk-seeking nor risk-averse behavior are inherently bad; that's determined by the context. There are numerous factors that determine when you should take on risk and when you should try to avoid it, including public opinion, cost, upside, and so on.

One of the characteristics that's associated with risk in daily fantasy sports is consistency. **The degree to which we can and should go against the grain is fundamentally related to predictability, which is governed by consistency. Remember, in a perfectly predictable world, there would be no incentive to ever be a contrarian.**

Baseball is the least predictable of all sports in the short-term, which I've described as a major advantage. In such a system, I think it behooves us to take more chances and really embrace a contrarian style of play. Unpredictability, if properly leveraged, is our best friend.

But not all aspects of MLB play are as unpredictable as others. While you're going to have a heck of a time predicting Mike Trout's home run total over the next 10 games, you can probably get pretty close to projecting Clayton Kershaw's strikeout count.

If you answered "at least a billion," you are correct.

Pitching stats are way, way more predictable than batting stats on the nightly level because of the difference in the sample size of relevant events (pitches thrown versus pitches seen). Pitchers have so many more opportunities for their play to regress toward their particular mean, which we've seen results in the pay-for-pitching strategy to make sense in both cash games and GPPs.

Since pitching is predictable and the elite arms are continually those that post the top DraftKings scores, it's a risk to fade the top pitchers in favor of cheaper options. It's not that such a move is never justified—I "semi-punt" one of my pitcher spots with some regularity—but doing so is "being greedy" when the long-term numbers suggest you should play it safe and pay for the top arms.

For me, pitcher selection is more of a "don't-fuck-this-up" type of deal than anything else. **My goal when placing pitchers into my lineup is generally to avoid risk. I don't really care all that much about value, and in fact, players like Kershaw will almost never be among the top values in a strict dollar-per-point sense because their cost makes it very difficult to "return value." However, I've never been a fan of analyzing players in this way because it 1) ignores probabilities and 2) treats players individually and not as one component of a broader picture.**

Regarding the first point, as mentioned, I don't care as much about maximizing the median projection of my lineup as I do about either increasing the floor or ceiling, depending on my goals. I'd rather maximize the probability of cashing by constructing my team in a specific way than to use a fragile value system to theoretically maximize points.

Further, when you pay up for a player like Kershaw, it obviously forces you to save money elsewhere, and those cheaper players are very likely to return value. So for me, **it isn't about a single player's projection or even their isolated probability of returning value, but rather the overall probability of the lineup as a whole performing as I'd like.**

Standing Tall Through Adversity

Throughout this book, I've made an effort to detail how I try to structure daily fantasy baseball teams that will benefit from chaos—antifragile lineups that excel when "things go wrong."

Antifragility is of course in opposition to fragility. A wine glass is fragile—it is harmed by volatility—while Skip Bayless's income is antifragile; the more we talk about that asshole, even if it's with complete disdain, the more he benefits.

In between those two extremes, though, is what Nassim Nicholas Taleb calls the "robust"—things that neither benefit nor are harmed by volatility. A diamond is an example of something that's robust; unlike a wine glass, it isn't harmed when you drop it (but it also doesn't benefit in any way). It's indifferent to chaos.

My goal when selecting pitchers is to be robust. I want consistency. I want predictability. I want pitchers on whom I can rely, even if the value isn't there in terms of projected

points and cost. The reason is that, due to the day-to-day consistency of pitchers, there's not as much of an opportunity to reap rewards from being antifragile. Yes, you stand to benefit if you fade Kershaw and King Felix on a day when they're highly owned but manage to tank—that's certainly antifragile—but the probability of that happening is incredibly low. Whereas even the best offenses in optimal situations can still be held to a run or two, the odds are much lower that the three most expensive pitchers will all turn in duds, for example.

I want my lineup as a whole to be antifragile, at least in tournaments, but that doesn't mean I need to be antifragile at every single spot. This is a similar concept to balancing value with usage; yes, a completely contrarian lineup stands to benefit immensely if all of the players perform well, but as you forgo greater levels of value, you're necessarily decreasing the chances of your lineup putting you in position to actually benefit. Even if you could guarantee a large GPP victory if all of your players return value, for example, it wouldn't be worth the struggle if the odds of that happening are 1-in-one-million.

Thus, my pitcher selection is very much about "staying in the game." I want a high enough floor from my arms to give my bats a chance to win it for me. In that way, **I take a cash-game-oriented strategy toward choosing pitchers and a GPP-oriented approach toward batters, regardless of the league type; I try to be fearful on pitchers when others are greedy and greedy on hitters when others are fearful.**

Start With the Arm(s)
When you're building a house, you can't just start with some weird-ass overhanging room in the upper level. You need to

create a foundation on which everything else can be built, and if your foundation is sloppy, the house will come crashing down and you won't be able to play daily fantasy sports for at least a couple days, which is sad.

I think the same idea is true in a number of areas. In business, rapid growth is often proceeded by a period of risk-averse foundation-building. In terms of personal wealth, it makes sense to minimize downside (by initially saving money, getting health insurance, and so on) before becoming more risk-seeking with different types of investments. Build a robust foundation now, when it's easy.

I take a similar approach to daily fantasy baseball lineup construction, typically starting the process with my arms. I might use three or four pitchers in a given day on DraftKings, mixing and matching different combinations, but I'd say I start with those guys in my lineup and build around them 90 percent of the time.

Once that robustness is in place, it's easier to take on risk with my bats without unnecessarily reducing the probability of a big score. And again, this difference in philosophy—when it's smart to seek risk and when it's not—boils down to positional consistency on a day-to-day basis.

Consistency Is King

Pitchers are clearly more consistent than batters from game to game, which is why allocating a large percentage of your salary cap to your two hurlers on DraftKings is smart; you're increasing your lineup's floor and upside at the same time.

Even within the pitcher position, though, there are different levels of consistency. **Outside of GB/FB rate, K/9 has proven**

to be the most consistent stat for pitchers—far more consistent than ERA, WHIP, and even BB/9.

That means that the flamethrowers who generally rack up a lot of Ks are also the most consistent types of pitchers. They rely on a consistent stat for fantasy production, not something that's rather volatile like earned runs or, worse, wins.

And which types of pitchers are the ones who generate a lot of strikeouts? The expensive ones, dummy. Thus, not only is it smart to pay top dollar for expensive pitchers because they're more reliable than hitters, but also because they're more reliable than other pitchers (not just in terms of bulk production, but rather in terms of how consistently they produce at specific rates).

Using the FanGraphs Stat Correlation Tool, I charted the correlation between various pitching stats from one year to the next (with the 'next' year being Year Y+1). The correlations that are in boxes are those for how well a specific stat predicts itself. How much does a pitcher's ERA carry over from year to year, for example? The data suggests not all that much…

	Year Y+1					
	ERA	WHIP	AVG	K/9	BB/9	GB/FB
ERA	0.311	0.304	0.307	-0.297	0.109	-0.032
WHIP	0.282	0.353	0.282	-0.281	0.237	0.073
AVG	0.306	0.282	0.42	-0.472	-0.081	0.133
K/9	-0.352	-0.32	-0.509	0.703	0.134	-0.211
BB/9	0.064	0.23	-0.093	0.16	0.544	-0.032
GB/FB	-0.066	0.057	0.118	-0.195	-0.034	0.752
xFIP	0.372	0.384	0.327	-0.422	0.222	-0.148
SIERA	0.417	0.412	0.418	-0.515	0.15	-0.07

There's a 0.311 strength of correlation between a pitcher's ERA from one year to the next, which isn't very strong.

Compare that to 0.703 for K/9, for example, or 0.752 for GB/FB. Pitchers who induce a lot of ground balls or whiff a lot of batters tend to do so every year, while a pitcher's ERA can fluctuate to a large degree.

I'm analyzing season-to-season numbers because I think they have usefulness on the nightly level. Yes, the odds of an individual hitter going deep or a single pitcher racking up 12 Ks isn't great in any given game, but if you're continually giving yourself exposure to the players with the highest probabilities of favorable outcomes—the players who are expected to produce over the long run—the variance will eventually even out. With daily fantasy baseball, you're just trying to assert those small edges here and there, night in and night out.

Going back to ERA, you can see that the best predictors of it, by far, have been xFIP and (in particular) SIERA. This is the reason I emphasize SIERA when analyzing my arms: it works. **When a pitcher's ERA is up early in the year but his SIERA is low, it suggests he isn't throwing the ball that poorly and that's probably a great time to buy low on him**. And vice versa, when the ERA is down but the SIERA is up, there's a good chance that DraftKings has that pitcher overpriced.

Note that K/9 is actually better than past ERA at predicting future ERA. The correlation between K/9 and ERA in Year Y+1 is -0.352. The negative value doesn't mean anything other than that as strikeouts increase, ERA decreases. So not only are strikeouts extremely consistent and a massive part of a pitcher's fantasy value, but they also predict success in other areas—like allowing runs—better than you might think. And if you look at batting average, you'll see that K/9 is actually the best predictor available, i.e. the most accurate way to predict a pitcher's future batting average allowed is to look at his strikeout rate.

We see similar effects across the board with pitcher stats, with SIERA and K/9 being the shit when it comes to making accurate predictions.

Maximizing Strikeout Probability

Okay, we want strikeouts. Got it. Now how the hell do we get them?

One way is to use astrology to target pitchers. I've always found that Libras start off the year really slowly, for example, and Pisces are unlikely to go nine full innings (they don't have long attention spans).

And don't even get me started on Scorpios!

A slightly more scientific way of predicting strikeouts is to use numbers. It's a crazy idea, I know; imagine picking your pitchers without even looking up their signs! (LOL, yeah right).

If you're going to insist on being a total dumbass and bypass astrology in favor of data, **you can use the K/9 for both a pitcher and the offense he's facing to project strikeouts**. For pitchers, I simply use their K/9 total from the previous season since the best predictor of future strikeouts is past strikeouts.

Then we need to adjust for the opponent. To do this, I calculate the K/9 for each batter in the lineup versus the handedness of the pitcher. So if we're projecting Kershaw against the Giants, I'd look at the strikeout rates for the Giants versus lefties—or more specifically, the total K/9 for each player in the lineup versus southpaws.

Then we have two numbers: a K/9 for the pitcher and a K/9 for the offense. Let's say that both of those numbers are 9.

You might think that you can project the pitcher at exactly nine strikeouts in that situation, but you'd be way off. We need to account for league baselines when projecting a stat like strikeouts.

Last season, offenses averaged 7.70 strikeouts per game—a number that continues to increase each and every season. Here's a look at total strikeouts per game from 2005 to 2014.

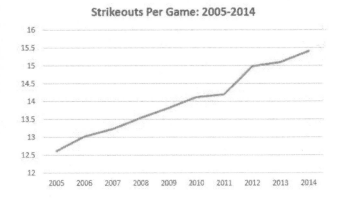

Strikeouts per game are up 22 percent since 2005, which is pretty insane. Here's a look at the increase in strikeouts per game since 2005.

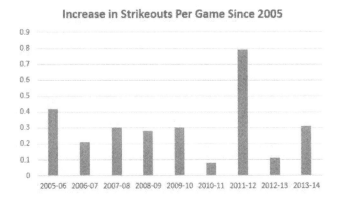

Based on recent trends, we should expect somewhere around 15.7 strikeouts per game in 2015 (or 7.85 per team). That's going to be our league baseline for strikeouts—7.85.

In the hypothetical game of a nine-strikeout pitcher versus a nine-strikeout offense, we have two inputs that are both greater than the league mean. So if we have a pitcher who records nine strikeouts per nine innings, on average, then we'd naturally project him above his average facing an offense that whiffs more than the typical team, right?

Of course. So here's how I do that:

Pitcher K/9 + Offense K/9 - Mean K/9

Add the pitcher's K/9 to the offense's K/9, then subtract the league mean K/9. In our hypothetical, that would be 9 + 9 - 7.85 = 10.15.

Note that the only time a pitcher's K/9 would match our projection for him would be if the opposing offense struck out at exactly the league average rate. This is a method, though imperfect, that I've found can help provide a nice baseline to predict strikeouts.

Of course, we're not actually using the K/9 totals as a strikeout projection since we'd never anticipate a pitcher going nine full innings in any single game. You can adjust the final K/9 total as you'd like based on the number of innings you think a pitcher might throw—obviously a guy like Strasburg and similar players have a tendency to get pulled early in games—but I find projecting innings to be pretty challenging on the day-to-day level.

Ultimately, the K/9 projections are more of a tool in our arsenal than an exact number on which we want to place a ton of emphasis. I care more about using K/9 to visualize upside and to rank pitchers according to strikeout probability than I do creating a fragile projection system.

A Basic Pitcher Ranking System

I've mentioned that I don't place much weight on very fine-tuned projections in daily fantasy baseball because of the variance inherent to the game. Instead, I take in as much information as I can, identifying stats I know are predictive and analyzing matchups, weather, lineup news, and other variables.

I think that such a strategy naturally sets itself up well for a ranking system, especially for pitchers since there aren't dozens of them to analyze each day. I think there are a few ways such a system can be configured, but one would be to rank pitchers in three categories: the Vegas projected run total for the opposing team, the K/9 calculation, and their SIERA.

Rank each pitcher in the three categories, take the average, and then re-rank and compare that to DraftKings salaries. If your No. 3-ranked pitcher is just the eighth-priciest on DraftKings, that's probably a good sign that he's a good value.

This isn't an exact process, but a decent way to find potential salary inefficiencies in a quick manner.

Ballparks, Weather, and Other Factors

Baseball is a binary sport, but that doesn't mean that our two-pronged approach to research needs to be separated. Actually, since the sport is zero-sum, almost everything uncovered when researching batters can be applied to pitchers, and vice versa. If you're projecting an offense to do really well in a given game, then you're almost necessarily predicting that the opposing picture will struggle.

That means that every part of the batter research from the previous chapter is applicable to pitchers, too. That includes park factors, weather, wOBA splits, home run probability, GB/FB ratios, and so on. It's all part of a larger collective—to predict the outcome of each game and then work down from there.

Having said that, I think the external factors probably don't matter as much for pitchers as for offenses. While an offense needs to hit the ball well for you to succeed—and thus is putting the ball into situations in which the weather and ballpark will have a big impact—a pitcher's goal is to not let the ball even get into play. If a pitcher is dealing, it doesn't matter all that much if it's 100 degrees or if the game is in a hitter-friendly park. Don't get me wrong—those are still things to consider—but if you're going to squeeze all of the upside that you can out of them, the external factors matter less than the matchup and how the pitcher is throwing.

Having said that, don't forget that one aspect of the weather—precipitation—matters a whole lot for pitchers. If the goal with pitchers is to secure reliable production, we can't take chances on pitchers in games with a serious threat of rain. Even if the game ultimately doesn't rain out, having a delay in the third or fourth inning will almost certainly result in your pitcher getting pulled, killing your lineup's upside.

Batted Ball Profiles

Major League Baseball is a game of competing minds, and like daily fantasy baseball tournaments, the "optimal" strategy depends on how others are thinking and behaving. Oakland's recent transition to an "all-we're-gonna-do-is-hit-the-ball-in-the-damn-air" offensive strategy is advantageous primarily because the rest of the league has targeted pitchers who induce ground balls. In terms of converting hits into runs, ground balls = bad for offenses.

Again, I think GB/FB rates are an important aspect of projecting hitters and pitchers that most daily fantasy baseball players overlook. Here's a look at the correlation between various batted ball profiles and offensive stats.

	GB/FB	GB%	FB%	LD%
BABIP	0.352	0.325	-0.468	0.472
wOBA	-0.241	-0.242	0.208	0.071
AB/HR	0.469	0.361	-0.398	0.156
ISO	-0.589	-0.566	0.625	-0.254

This is one reason that, although there's a ton of variance with BABIP, some players—namely those who hit a lot of ground balls—will naturally have a higher BABIP. **As ground ball percentage (GB%) increases, so does BABIP.**

I think this might be one reason that ground balls have been so overrated in the past; they lead to positive outcomes more often than fly balls. However, when fly balls are beneficial to offenses, they're typically *really* beneficial. In that way, fly balls are sort of antifragile relative to ground balls—benefiting from variance (a wind gust, a short porch in right field, high temperatures, etc).

Fly balls are easy to catch, and thus lead to more extreme outcomes than ground balls (very often a binary home-run-or-out result). But take a look at the correlation between hitters' ground ball and fly ball rates versus their wOBA, AB/HR, and ISO; they're all very much in favor of fly ball percentage. **As a hitter's fly ball rate increases, his wOBA and ISO do the same, while the number of at-bats he needs per home run unsurprisingly decreases**. For ground ball hitters, it's the exact opposite—lower wOBA and ISO, and more at-bats per dinger.

The ISO correlations in particular are pretty astonishing. Remember, ISO is a simple measure of raw power—something that's really important for daily fantasy baseball upside—and fly ball hitters have been astonishingly more powerful than ground ball hitters.

This data suggests that you should be targeting primarily ground ball pitchers to reduce downside, specifically against bats that are unlikely to put the ball into the air at a high rate.

Pitcher Scoring Based on Salary and Ownership

When we're trying to discern an individual player's value, there are a few really crucial components, the two most important of which are scarcity and consistency; **everything else equal, we want players who we can't reproduce—those who are outliers at their positions—as well as those whose production we can predict with a reasonable degree of accuracy**.

We can get some sense of scarcity by examining the average DraftKings production of pitchers, broken down by salary and ownership.

			Percentile of Salary		
			Top Third	**Middle Third**	**Bottom Third**
Percentile of Ownership		**Top Third**	19.6	16.3	15.4
		Middle Third	15.7	13.9	13.3
		Bottom Third	13.5	12.4	10.3

Here's a different look at this data...

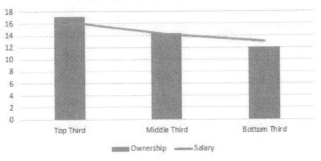

The top third of pitchers in terms of ownership outproduce the top third in terms of salary, which I think speaks to the level of predictability at the position. That consistency is linked to pricing; you don't need to pay for the top arms *because* they're expensive, but rather because their predictability is the impetus for them being priced in the top tier. Basically, DraftKings is more likely to "get it right" with their pitcher pricing due to the nightly consistency at the position. It's fine to drop into the middle tier and even the bottom tier of pricing at times, but it's simply less likely you're going to find a high floor and/or ceiling in that range as compared to batters. It's more obvious when a high-value pitcher is priced outside of the top tier than it is with batters, but it's just less likely to occur.

Looking solely at the top two tiers of ownership, here's another measure of scarcity, broken down by salary.

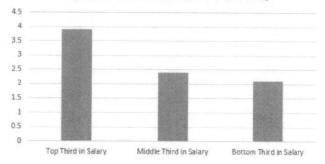

More evidence to not fade the chalk. There's a higher level of scarcity within the top tier of pitchers, i.e. the difference between the "obvious" pitcher plays and the not-so-obvious ones is greatest among the most expensive arms. **If you're going to use a moderately priced pitcher, there's less incentive to conform to public opinion—less reason to play the chalk (outside of very obvious errors in pricing)— because those pitchers aren't as predictable as the top arms.**

When to Go Cheap at Pitcher

I think it's important to make sure you don't pigeonhole yourself into any particular no-matter-what sort of strategy. When in doubt, you should use general heuristics based on long-term data, but there are many times when heuristics don't apply or when there's enough contradicting evidence to go in the opposite direction. So **"pay for pitching" is a good rule of thumb, but not an everlasting doctrine**.

If you're blindly selecting mid- and bottom-tier pitchers, though, you're going to be in trouble. Here are some traits that I emphasize when I decide to save a little money on one (or sometimes both) of my arms.

High K/9

A lot of the high-strikeout pitchers are among the most expensive, but there are always a handful of hurlers who sit down batters with regularity, but don't otherwise have elite stuff (at least not consistently). Young pitchers who make batters miss but struggle with control at times, for example, can give you strikeout upside at a cheap price.

The good part about K/9 is that it's extremely consistent. With a high-strikeout pitcher, your job is less about figuring out if he'll whiff hitters—he usually will for as long as he's in the game—and more about determining if he can rack up enough innings to realize his potential.

I almost never roster a cheap pitcher if he doesn't have high upside in terms of Ks.

Extreme Splits (GB/FB, L/R)

As mentioned, platoon splits are an easy and effective way to find value. When a player has extreme splits in either direction, his matchups probably aren't completely priced into his salary. A southpaw who is nasty versus left-handed bats and will be facing a primarily left-handed lineup, for example, will often offer value.

In addition to lefty/righty splits, I also look at batted ball profiles. Remember, ground ball hitters struggle mightily against ground ball pitchers. **GB/FB rates are highly unlikely to be factored into pricing on daily fantasy sites, so you can**

sometimes get a deal on a mid-tier pitcher with a favorable matchup in terms of batted ball profiles.

An Unavoidable Stack

I usually begin my lineup creation with pitchers, then move to my favorite stack(s), and then fill in the value bats. But sometimes there's a particular offensive stack that I really want to target, in which case I'll build around those players.

If that stack is one that costs a pretty penny, I'll occasionally try extra hard to find an affordable arm so that I can get the bats I want into my lineup. That's particularly true when an expensive stack—like the Blue Jays, Tigers, Angels, etc—is in a perceived poor matchup. If I can get upside without high ownership, I'm going to take it.

Start of Season

Daily fantasy pricing tends to fluctuate more at the start of the season than any other time; people overreact to a small sample size of data, and thus you're more likely to find a quality arm at an affordable price in May than you are in September.

This is where understanding randomness comes into play. I use the same stats as with my batters—HR/FB, BABIP, and so on—to determine how "lucky" a pitcher has been. If we're looking at a pitcher who has succeeded in the past but has a high HR/FB and BABIP to start the season (and preferably a SIERA that's lower than his ERA), then there's a good chance he has unnecessarily dropped in price.

Short Slates

During very short slates, you're going to see massive usage on certain pitchers. If you're semi-confident in a pitcher who you believe is going to fly under the radar, it can make sense to take a flier on a guy whose lowered usage will make up for his reduced probability of returning value. I still generally side with the top-priced arms in short slates, but I'd say **I'm slightly more likely to be contrarian with at least one pitcher in a three-game slate than a 12-game slate**.

Vegas

Finally, I'll always take a second look at a player that Vegas really likes. If a mid-priced pitcher is -200 to win a game and has a favorable strikeout prop, I'll generally trust that the wise guys in Vegas have it right.

DraftKings generally has astute pitcher pricing, but no one is as accurate as Vegas over the long run. **If my own research matches what Vegas thinks, that's even more incentive to bite the bullet and fade the most expensive pitchers**.

CSURAM88's Analysis

Again, I'm going to let Vegas do most of my research for me when it comes to pitchers. You can learn so much just from monitoring the run totals and strikeout props for starting pitchers. If a pitcher is facing a team with a really low projected run total, that's a good sign that he's going to have a quality outing.

Whereas I don't fade batters who have struggled in the recent past, I will sometimes do that with pitchers (or target those who are on a roll). The numbers suggest that pitchers are more likely than hitters to have their performance from one game carry into the next. It all comes down to sample sizes, which help us know if a pitcher's recent performance is reflective of how well he's actually throwing.

I also like to look at how a pitcher's strikeouts and WHIP, for example, match up with his recent fantasy production. Sometimes a pitcher will string together three quality starts with seven-plus innings of work, but he just didn't strike out a ton of batters. If that's someone we can normally count on for Ks, he might be underpriced. Also, it matters if a pitcher has been getting consistently hit hard or if he had maybe just one blow-up inning that has thrown off his stats over his last few starts.

And as is the case with hitters, I consider the ballpark when selecting my arms. When a pitcher from a really hitter-friendly park travels somewhere where the ball doesn't carry as well or that is otherwise pitcher-friendly, he'll get a boost. But that's not as large of a factor as the weather or some other variables since Vegas can properly account for the ballpark; it's a static input into their model.

At the end of the day, though, it just comes down to minimizing as much risk as possible with pitchers, regardless of the league type. I usually pay top-dollar for the best pitchers, even if they aren't the best values, because it's so important to me to acquire that consistent source of production.

"In baseball, you don't know nothing."

Yogi Berra

VI. Data, So Hot Right Now, Data

"It is a capital mistake to theorize before one has data."

Arthur Conan Doyle

This has been fun, hasn't it? I love using numbers to explain complex events and aid in predicting the future, so I hope you've enjoyed the first five chapters.

Prior to writing the book, I spent a few weeks just looking crap up. At one point, my girlfriend asked me "Is our relationship going to end because of Excel?" and I babbled something about there being no correlation between the two.

A little nerd humor, you know.

Anyway, prior to doing research, I create some sort of hypothesis based on hunches or things I think I see in games. While I don't think that "grinding film" or watching games is useless, I think it's really easy to get fooled by randomness from individual games. Even if you watch every game you can, you're inevitably going to have some plays that stand out in your mind, for whatever reason, that end up skewing your perception. **I use data as a way to confirm or debunk the narratives my mind inevtiably creates**.

Some people might argue that going into research with a specific hypothesis in mind can end up ruining how the data is collected or presented. I think this is a very real issue—one that I try my hardest to avoid—but I also think it's unrealistic and impractical to not form hypotheses when watching sports. Even if that hypothesis is as simple as "Andy Dalton sucks," you'll always have natural inclinations.

So I go into research maybe leaning one way or another in terms of how I believe things might turn out, but I never set artificial parameters to help prove my case. Ultimately, this results in a lot of data that either suggests what I believed is false, or else data that's just sort of neutral.

In any event, this chapter is a collection of data that, for whatever reason, just didn't make its way into the other chapters. I think that some of it is interesting but not actionable (such as the most valuable individual MLB players on DraftKings), some of it is time-sensitive (such as which teams had the largest discrepancy in lefty/righty splits from last season), and some of it is data from DraftKings that I just wanted to save until the end because it rocks.

As an author, I need to start my books strong and end them strong. Those are the two key elements. I can't be like pancakes: all exciting at first but by the end you're fucking sick of 'em.

So without further ado, here's my appendix of extra data, sorted into "General MLB" and "DraftKings-Specific."

General MLB Data

I collected the majority of this data on either Baseball Reference or FanGraphs. Baseball is unique in that a lot of the research we conduct on the sport—what works and predicts success for MLB teams—can be applied directly to fantasy baseball. Everything is standardized in a way that a sport like football, with different schemes and team philosophies, is not.

Power Lefty/Righty Offensive Splits By Team

I'm obviously a huge proponent of breaking numbers down into buckets of relevant players, with the most important and useful of those being simple lefty/righty splits. Whether it's wOBA, ISO, or whatever, everything needs to be broken down based on handedness.

One idea I had was to break down which offenses in baseball are the most "extreme" based on handedness. That is, which have the biggest differences in their production based on if the pitcher is a lefty or a righty?

I charted the differences in three different stats—ISO, AB/HR, and fly ball percentage—based on the opposing pitcher's handedness. I chose those three stats because they're clear predictors of home runs. The idea is that offenses that have extreme results against a certain handedness of pitcher can perhaps offer value because their overall stats won't represent their upside (and downside) versus specific types of pitchers.

The first stat is ISO.

	ISO vs L	ISO vs R	Difference (L-R)
Rangers	0.14	0.111	0.029
Cardinals	0.134	0.11	0.024
Brewers	0.164	0.142	0.022
Tigers	0.166	0.144	0.022
Rockies	0.184	0.163	0.021
Reds	0.143	0.123	0.02
Phillies	0.133	0.117	0.016
Red Sox	0.134	0.121	0.013
Orioles	0.175	0.163	0.012
Rays	0.128	0.117	0.011
White Sox	0.153	0.143	0.01
Braves	0.127	0.117	0.01
Royals	0.121	0.111	0.01
Angels	0.153	0.145	0.008
Astros	0.146	0.139	0.007
Dodgers	0.139	0.141	-0.002
Cubs	0.144	0.146	-0.002
Giants	0.131	0.134	-0.003
Yankees	0.132	0.136	-0.004
Diamondbacks	0.121	0.129	-0.008
Marlins	0.117	0.127	-0.01
Athletics	0.129	0.14	-0.011
Nationals	0.131	0.143	-0.012
Padres	0.106	0.119	-0.013
Twins	0.125	0.141	-0.016
Blue Jays	0.142	0.16	-0.018
Mets	0.098	0.134	-0.036
Indians	0.108	0.148	-0.04
Pirates	0.111	0.154	-0.043
Mariners	0.102	0.148	-0.046

The teams listed at the top—the Rangers, Cardinals, Brewers, Tigers, and Rockies—had the largest difference in success between lefties and righties (they were the most superior against southpaws). The teams listed at the bottom—the Mariners, Pirates, Indians, Mets, and Blue Jays—crushed right-handed pitching much more so than lefties.

Next up is AB/HR…

	AB/HR vs L	AB/HR vs R	Difference (L-R)
Royals	47.9	63.4	-15.5
Rangers	39.7	54.1	-14.4
Cardinals	42.2	56.0	-13.9
Phillies	38.8	47.8	-9.0
Brewers	30.6	38.6	-8.0
Braves	38.8	46.5	-7.7
Reds	35.7	43.2	-7.5
Rockies	25.3	32.5	-7.2
Tigers	33.0	37.7	-4.7
White Sox	32.8	37.0	-4.2
Dodgers	39.0	42.4	-3.4
Red Sox	43.0	46.1	-3.2
Rays	45.1	47.9	-2.8
Orioles	25.4	26.9	-1.6
Angels	35.4	36.9	-1.5
Athletics	37.4	38.2	-0.8
Astros	32.9	33.6	-0.8
Cubs	34.5	35.3	-0.7
Padres	51.0	47.8	3.2
Diamondbacks	49.5	46.3	3.2
Yankees	40.1	36.4	3.7
Blue Jays	34.8	30.3	4.5
Giants	45.1	40.4	4.7
Marlins	51.3	43.9	7.3
Nationals	42.7	34.6	8.1
Twins	53.1	40.0	13.1
Mets	58.6	40.6	18.0
Pirates	52.3	32.6	19.8
Indians	56.7	34.4	22.4
Mariners	68.3	32.8	35.6

This list isn't terribly different. Again, we see the Rangers, Cardinals, and Brewers in the top five (best against lefties), as well as the Mariners, Indians, Pirates, and Mets in the bottom five (superior versus righties). The Mariners, in particular, had serious trouble going deep against lefties.

And finally, here's a look at FB%...

	FB% vs L	FB% vs R	Difference (L-R)
Tigers	38.1%	34.7%	3.4%
Brewers	36.9%	34.5%	2.4%
Rangers	33.2%	31.3%	1.9%
Cardinals	33.5%	31.8%	1.7%
Rays	36.1%	34.6%	1.5%
Red Sox	36.2%	34.7%	1.5%
Marlins	31.8%	30.5%	1.3%
Angels	35.0%	33.7%	1.3%
Blue Jays	36.5%	35.3%	1.2%
Mets	37.6%	36.4%	1.2%
Dodgers	31.7%	30.9%	0.8%
Giants	36.0%	35.3%	0.7%
White Sox	32.9%	33.0%	-0.1%
Diamondbacks	31.6%	31.8%	-0.2%
Indians	34.8%	35.2%	-0.4%
Twins	34.8%	35.2%	-0.4%
Rockies	32.3%	33.1%	-0.8%
Astros	35.8%	36.7%	-0.9%
Pirates	33.9%	34.9%	-1.0%
Phillies	32.5%	33.5%	-1.0%
Nationals	32.6%	34.6%	-2.0%
Padres	29.7%	31.7%	-2.0%
Yankees	33.5%	35.6%	-2.1%
Orioles	35.5%	37.6%	-2.1%
Braves	31.6%	33.9%	-2.3%
Royals	30.3%	33.0%	-2.7%
Mariners	32.6%	35.5%	-2.9%
Athletics	38.8%	42.0%	-3.2%
Reds	32.6%	35.9%	-3.3%
Cubs	31.8%	38.8%	-7.0%

Holy shit Cubbies. The offense that had the second-highest overall fly ball rate in baseball last season was way, way worse against left-handed pitching. Actually, it was more than twice the differential than any other team in the league. That data suggests the Cubs might hit fewer home runs per at-bat versus southpaws next year. Also, check out the Athletics' fly ball rate—through the roof against both lefties and righties.

I ranked each team in each of the three stats to get their average rank…

	Average Rank
Rangers	2.0
Cardinals	3.0
Brewers	3.3
Tigers	4.7
Red Sox	8.7
Rays	9.3
Rockies	10.0
Phillies	10.3
White Sox	11.3
Angels	12.3
Dodgers	12.7
Royals	13.3
Reds	14.0
Braves	14.3
Orioles	15.7
Astros	16.7
Marlins	17.3
Giants	17.7
Diamondbacks	18.0
Blue Jays	19.0
Yankees	21.0
Mets	21.3
Cubs	21.7
Padres	21.7
Athletics	22.0
Twins	22.3
Nationals	23.0
Indians	24.0
Pirates	25.3
Mariners	29.0

Again, the teams at the top are those that were not necessarily the best against lefties, but rather the best versus lefties relative to their overall performance (so a below-average offense that was average against lefties would probably offer value versus southpaws relative to their overall cost).

Obviously there are some limitations, most notably that rosters change. Still, there's enough turnover from year to year that you can get a sense of which offenses are the most likely to be far superior versus either lefties or righties.

You can also perform this sort of analysis during the season to see which current teams are outliers in one direction or the other. We're looking for offenses at either end of the spectrum—either far superior versus lefties or righties than vice versa—to help uncover value.

In terms of 2014, the five most powerful offenses versus southpaws relative to their overall performance were the Rangers, Cardinals, Brewers, Tigers, and Red Sox, while the five offenses with the most righty-skewed power stats were the Mariners, Pirates, Indians, Nationals, and Twins.

Age-Based Data

Age-based data has the most use in season-long leagues—particularly dynasty formats—but I still think there's some value in it for daily fantasy baseball. Specifically, aging data can help determine how probable it is that early-season trends continue; is the aging pitcher who starts the season horribly going to improve, or are the early-season results his new norm?

Here's a look at strikeouts per nine innings for all pitchers since 2010.

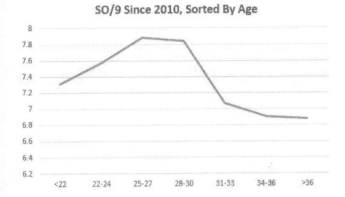

SO/9 Since 2010, Sorted By Age

In terms of strikeouts, pitchers tend to steadily climb from the moment they enter the league until around ages 25 to 27, where they peak as a whole. They continue that rate of production until their early-30s, when strikeout rate tends to fall dramatically.

I think it's useful to know that there's probably a far greater difference between a 27-year-old pitcher and a 32-year-old hurler than a 32-year-old pitcher and a 37-year-old. Once pitchers lose some of their power, they're forced to get creative and use intelligent pitch location to beat batters—traits they can presumably maintain for a decent amount of time.

We see a somewhat similar aging curve for batters in terms of home run rates.

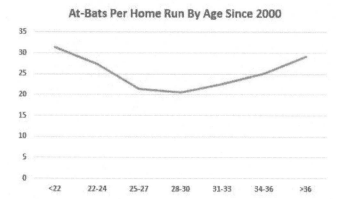

The lower the number, the fewer at-bats needed per home run, and thus the greater the power. Note that we might expect the power for current batters in their mid-30s to tail off more than we've seen. I studied every hitter since 2000, which of course includes some dudes who might or might not have been hitting baseballs twice as far as they should have.

Completely unrelated, but for the record, I think the idea of Barry Bonds getting snubbed from the Hall of Fame is asinine. Just a completely ridiculous decision made by the same type of people who would punt on 4th-and-1 in opponent territory and won't have sex with the lights on.

To be honest, I'm not terribly bullish on lights-on sex either, but whatevs.

Pitch Types

File this data under "Interesting, maybe useful, but probably not." Here's a look at the correlation between four stats and the rate of four different types of pitches—fastballs, curveballs, changeups, and sliders.

	FB%	CB%	CH%	SL%
K/9	-0.038	0.137	-0.004	0.066
HR/9	-0.206	-0.016	0.17	-0.039
xFIP	0.087	-0.126	0.05	-0.044
WHIP	0.174	-0.006	-0.066	-0.048

None of these correlations are particularly strong, with that between FB% and HR/9 being the strongest (and a negative correlation). That is, the more fastballs a pitcher throws, the less likely he is to get taken deep. I found this to be sort of interesting—actually the opposite of what I naturally assumed—so I broke down home run rates by fastball percentage.

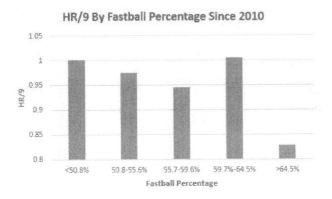

It turns out that most fastball pitchers are as likely as anyone else to give up home runs, but the true flamethrowers—the guys throwing heat at least 64.5 percent of the time (usually pitchers who throw really hard)—aren't getting taken yard as often as everyone else.

Again, this is tough to apply on the individual level outside of perhaps taking a careful look at a pitcher's HR/9, HR/FB, and other power numbers if he throws serious gas.

Total Base Upside

I'm clearly fascinated with game theory's role in daily fantasy sports tournament success, and I think that's really the next frontier of research. I tried to provide some cool data on ownership and how that matches up with production/upside.

I think it's natural to dismiss game theory or a contrarian style of play and say, "Well you just need to pick the best players." That's a naïve view, in my opinion, because it totally ignores probabilities and the potential benefits of actually selecting the most high-value players.

I always like to use extreme examples when attempting to demonstrate a point, and the hypothetical of a player or stack being 100 percent owned does a nice job of showing the absurdity of ignoring player utilization. If the Rockies were such a good play at home one night that literally everyone played the same stack, then no one would benefit or be hurt by whatever happened to those players; they could collectively hit 25 home runs or strike out 25 times, and it just wouldn't matter.

If you were the sole player who faded that stack, you'd be in a sensational position if the Rockies tank; if you were in a 100-man GPP and 99 users rostered the Rockies, you'd basically win the thing if they fail to score, for example (or even if your stack outscores them and you don't fuck up your pitching).

In that scenario, you'd only need to be "right"—you'd only need for the chalk to disappoint—more than one percent of the time for you to benefit. If Colorado had just one bad game in 10, for example, you'd still be in a wonderful spot given that you'd surge past a field of 99 users in 10 percent of games. Anyone else interested in winning 10 percent of GPPs?

At the other end of the spectrum, imagine that 99 daily fantasy players had their heads up their asses and failed to roster the Rockies in a quality matchup at home. If you were the only user to play a Colorado stack, you'd benefit immensely from rostering high-value players without a heavy level of ownership. Whereas Colorado going off in the first scenario would put Rockies owners ahead of just one percent of the field, the same in the second scenario would put the lone Rockies owner ahead of all 99 other users.

It follows that player utilization matters—a lot—and that there's a balance that we need to strike between finding value and still getting away from high-usage situations when it's appropriate. That's particularly true in baseball because, due to stacking, there's a ton of lineup overlap.

The point at which value and usage "balance out" depends on how accurately we can predict the future. In a previous chapter, I mentioned that if we could predict the future with 100 percent accuracy, it would never make sense to go against the grain. But we can't, so we should.

BUT, the frequency with which we should be contrarian (and the level of "contrarianism" we're willing to take on) depends on the level of certainty we can have in game outcomes and player results. If the Rockies theoretically finished as the top fantasy offense 90 percent of the time when they're projected above, say, 5.5 runs, that would make it much more challenging to fade them in such a situation than if they're the top fantasy offense just 10 percent of the time, for example.

So instead of working with just pure value in a vacuum, there are really three factors at play here: value, the consistency with which we can properly identify that value, and the benefits we'll receive if we're correct in identifying that value.

As the ability to make accurate predictions decreases, the value of fading the chalk increases dramatically. And, as we've seen, baseball is a highly volatile sport from night to night, which is again the main impetus for my stance on going against the grain.

Thus, it's imperative to look at how frequently we can predict value—or perhaps more important, how consistently we can identify upside, since that's what is needed to win GPPs. Stacking the Padres or Royals might be contrarian as hell, but it could also be useless if they don't have the requisite upside to consistently give you a fighting change in a large tournament.

With that said, here's a look at the probability of offenses reaching 20 or 25 total bases.

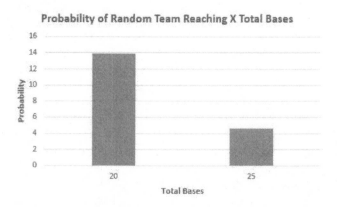

This is a very basic measure of upside. I chose total bases because that's a decent proxy for overall fantasy production. It turns out that MLB offenses record 20 total bases or more in around 14 percent of games (one in seven or so), but they reach 25 total bases much less frequently at close to five percent (one in 20 games, or close to three times less often).

We're looking for that really rare 25-total-base type of production in GPPs. Here's how often each team reached that mark in 2014.

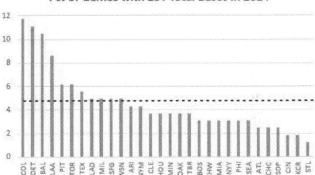

It's not surprising to see Colorado at the top of the list, leading all teams with 25-plus total bases in just under 12 percent of games—well over twice the league average. That mark is also many times more frequent than the least explosive offense—the St. Louis Cardinals.

I marked the league average with dashes, and you can see that only 11 teams checked in above that average, four of them just barely. Only six offenses exceeded the average rate of 25-plus total bases by more than one percentage point, and only four did it by more than two.

To me, **these numbers are more evidence that we can and should fade the obvious offenses in certain situations, but we can't go completely off the map; we still need offenses capable of going deep and giving us the sort of upside needed to win a large GPP**.

That means fading the Tigers in a plus matchup is fine, but it's not like you can roll the Royals or Cardinals out there and expect to win with consistency. Instead, it's the teams that are a combination of high-upside and moderate-usage—like the Pirates and Brewers (two teams that led to a lot of GPP success last year, by the way)—that are probably the best long-term GPP plays.

There are times when it's too juicy of a matchup to fade the Rockies playing at Coors Field, but when you do it, you should still be rostering offenses with plenty of upside, balancing value with utilization to acquire the best of both worlds.

DraftKings Data

In the 19th century, scientists noticed that the planet Mercury has a strange wobble in its orbit, and they hypothesized the existence of a planet—named Vulcan—that existed between Mercury and the sun. Vulcan's belief was widely accepted until a young man named Albert came along in 1915 with his fancy "Theory of Relativity" and explained how space's curvature would cause Mercury to orbit the sun in a strange manner.

Einstein's theory was simpler than Vulcan (it didn't need to assume the existence of an entire planet), it fit better with current beliefs (mainly that a fucking planet that no one ever saw existed next to the sun), and it could explain other phenomenon outside of Mercury's orbit, so it was a much better theory.

This is how science works: scientists create theories based on observed phenomena, they search for evidence to confirm or falsify those theories, and ultimately the best theory—the one that makes the fewest independent assumptions, fits with other beliefs we consider to be true, explains the widest range of observations, and makes the most accurate predictions—wins out.

The Vulcan theory turned out to be wrong, but lots of similar theories did not; evidence once pointed to the existence of atoms, subatomic particles, and black holes, for example, even though they had never been observed. Today, many physicists believe in the existence of white holes—the opposite of a black hole as a region of spacetime that spits out matter and light, but cannot be entered from the outside—yet one has never been observed.

The idea I'm getting at is that we're always constructing theories based on the evidence we have, but those theories need to be flexible as we obtain new evidence. One of the reasons I've been so pleased to work with DraftKings on the creation of my books is because they've been able to provide daily fantasy players with evidence to help confirm or debunk the merits of specific strategies and philosophies.

It's one thing to theorize about which sorts of strategies *should* lead to daily fantasy success, but another altogether to actually see which lineup construction and game selection philosophies are *actually* winning leagues. It's been incredible that DraftKings has opened their doors to daily fantasy players, and I'm honored to be the messenger.

Basically, they're letting us pull back the curtain so that we know which of our unconfirmed theories have some basis in reality and which ones are the equivalent of Vulcan.

Ownership and Game Start Time

If GPP success is about balancing value with ownership, it makes sense that we need to consider how consistently we can accurately project those two traits. Ownership might matter a whole heck of a lot, but it doesn't matter if we can't predict it with any sort of reliability—similar to how hot streaks might exist but it doesn't matter if we can't predict them.

I think there are a number of ways to predict player ownership with decent accuracy. **The Vegas lines—which can turn into a reflection of public opinion in baseball—are an accurate proxy for team ownership. There's also generally higher usage on the chalk in tournaments with high buy-ins, while tournaments with lower buy-ins—those with a lot more weaker players—are less about value; novice users generally aren't very price-sensitive.**

Another way to predict player usage is to simply look at a game's start time. When I worked with DraftKings on the data for this book, I asked them to look into how player ownership was distributed based on the game time. My hypothesis was that we'd see lower-than-expected player usage in late games.

Here's a look at the percentage of batters rostered at 7pm, 8pm, 9pm, and 10pm EST.

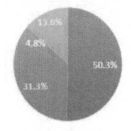

Actual Percentage of Batters Rostered By Game Time

■ 7pm   ■ 8pm   ■ 9pm   ■ 10pm

This data alone doesn't mean much because we need to set some sort of expectation. Obviously we'd expect the highest usage in the 7pm slot because that's when most games begin. So I charted expected utilization based on game start time.

Expected Percentage of Batters Rostered By Game Time

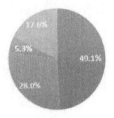

■ 7pm ■ 8pm ■ 9pm ■ 10pm

You might argue that fewer players are rostered in late games because the West Coast offenses aren't as good as some that play elsewhere in the country, but I don't think that's true. The Angels, A's, and Rockies are all explosive offenses that ranked in the top five in usage last season, and all play late games when at home.

I subtracted actual usage from expected usage to see where the largest discrepancies are located.

Difference in Actual Versus Expected Player Usage By Game Time

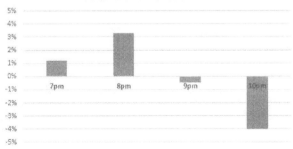

It's pretty amazing that, based on the number of games in the 10pm EST slot, we'd expect 17.6 percent usage but see only 13.6 percent. That's a massive drop, and thus a really big inefficiency that we can potentially exploit.

So why are people fading the late games more than we'd expect? I think there are two factors at play. The first is that there are simply fewer daily fantasy players who follow the teams on the West Coast. People naturally like to root for teams they like (or at least those they can watch on TV), and so they don't roster players in the late games as often.

The second—perhaps the more influential—is that we often don't have lineup cards for the 10pm EST games by the time contests begin on DraftKings around 7pm EST. It's of course ideal to know a team's lineup before rostering their players, and so a lot of users probably fade the late games due to uncertainty.

If you're willing to monitor lineups and use the late-swap feature on DraftKings, though, I think it makes sense to target players in 10pm EST games as much as possible. You can generally predict the lineup with a decent level of accuracy, anyway, and the uncertainty that might result from the lineup being unavailable at contest lock isn't as much of a problem on DraftKings as it is on some other daily fantasy sites—and, as is a clear theme of this book, I'd argue the uncertainty can be leveraged into an advantage.

Ownership and Streaky Play
Another tactic you can use to help you predict ownership is to understand how recent performance affects public perception. The crowd loves to jump on players who are "hot," even if their price has risen. Take a look at the average

DraftKings ownership on players based on how many consecutive games they have produced above their personal average in fantasy points.

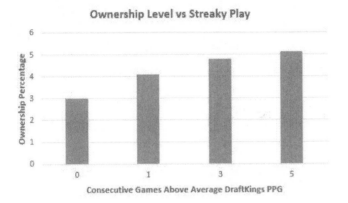

Coming off of a single game below their average—the 'zero' category here—players average 3.0 percent usage in tournaments. With just one above-average game, that number jumps to 4.1 percent—36.7 percent higher than just one game prior. At three straight games with above-average production, average player usage is 4.8 percent, and it's 5.1 percent with five straight games of superb play.

The biggest jump comes after just a single game of quality play. **Daily fantasy players seem quick to react to what they perceive as "streaky" play, so in terms of ownership, you can become more contrarian by focusing on bats coming off of at least one day of below-average production**.

Home and Away Production

While researching for this book, I asked my Twitter followers what sort of data they'd like to see, and fellow DraftKings Pro

Dinkpiece said he was interested in seeing home versus away fantasy scoring. So this one's for you, Drew.

Baseball is unique in that away teams are guaranteed an opportunity at as much production as they can muster before generating 27 outs, while home teams are guaranteed just 24 outs (assuming the game isn't rained out).

If home teams always won and never got to bat in the bottom of the ninth inning, they'd have just 88.9 percent as many outs as road teams. Of course, home teams don't always win, so the overall number is closer to 94 percent. Still, it's something.

Of course, home teams also play slightly better than road teams, too, due to a variety of factors (travel, ballpark familiarity, umpire biases, etc). So do these factors "cancel out," or should we expect more long-term fantasy production from either road or home teams?

	Avg Total Score for Batters	St Dev of Total Score for Batters
Home Teams	59.6	29.0
Away teams	60.1	27.1

Overall, **home teams haven't made up for the reduced plate appearances, though the numbers are close; they've produced 99.2 percent of the fantasy production of away teams**. That's a result that's close enough that we probably can't place too much emphasis on targeting away teams solely because they're on the road.

However, there are two situations in which I think it makes sense to give road offenses a small boost. The first is if DraftKings underprices players who are on away teams. If road stacks as a whole are cheaper than home stacks, then you should obviously target the away players if you expect production to be equal.

Second, **this could be evidence to be bullish on away players in cash games**. If you look at the standard deviation of scores for home/away batters, you see that **road teams are less volatile; the guaranteed plate appearances increase the safety of teams on the road**, which is of course a beneficial feature for your 50/50 and heads-up lineups.

It might be a small effect, but I'd probably side with road players/stacks in cash games whenever you're undecided.

Stacking Data

One of the central themes of this book is that maximizing projected points—which can be done by almost always playing the chalk—is an overrated daily fantasy strategy. Sometimes your philosophy should closely resemble point-maximization, but sometimes not.

I used data on ownership and points needed to win a GPP to display that point. Here's some more stacking data that lends credence to the idea that, while points matter, they shouldn't be your only focus. Take a look at the top 10 offenses from last season in terms of points scored with stacks of four-plus players.

Team Stacked	Avg Points	% GPPs Won	% of LUs which Won
Colorado	107.5	5.4%	0.38%
Los Angeles	104.0	2.7%	0.26%
Miami	103.3	1.5%	0.28%
Baltimore	100.0	3.0%	0.27%
Washington	100.0	2.1%	0.23%
Atlanta	99.4	1.4%	0.19%
Cleveland	99.0	2.0%	0.16%
Arizona	98.6	1.5%	0.28%
Milwaukee	98.1	4.0%	0.40%
Pittsburgh	97.4	2.2%	0.20%

Not surprising to see Colorado lead the list. **When DraftKings users rostered at least four Rockies players, they averaged 107.5 points**. Typically rostered at home, Colorado stacks had the obvious benefit of playing at Coors Field. Because of their popularity, Rockies stacks won 5.4 percent of all GPPs—more than any other team.

As I've tried to demonstrate, though, there's a difference between the chances of a particular stack winning a tournament and the odds of *you* winning if you roster that stack; we need to account for how frequently each team/player is utilized. If the Rockies were theoretically stacked in 20 percent of lineups, that 5.4 percent win rate would be awful, for example. If they were in only two percent of lineups, it would be sensational. It's all about how usage matches up with results.

For example, you can see that **the Brewers—a team that won fewer GPPs and scored 9.4 fewer points than the**

Rockies, on average—actually led to more GPP success; if you rostered a Milwaukee stack last season, you had a 0.40 percent chance to win a GPP, which was slightly higher than Colorado.

There's clearly a relationship between points and GPP success, but it isn't as tight as you might think. The success of some of the "worst" offenses in baseball is more evidence of that.

Team Stacked	Avg Points	% GPPs Won	% of LUs which Won
Philadelphia	92.0	1.1%	0.27%
Seattle	92.1	0.9%	0.28%
Texas	92.9	0.4%	0.09%
Boston	92.9	0.6%	0.12%
NY Yankees	93.1	1.6%	0.20%
Chi WS	93.2	0.7%	0.10%
St. Louis	93.4	1.5%	0.19%
Cincinnati	93.6	1.4%	0.21%
San Diego	94.0	1.3%	0.18%
Chi Cubs	94.4	0.2%	0.06%

The Phillies scored a league-low 92.0 fantasy points when users stacked them, yet you still had a 0.27 percent chance to take down a tournament with a Philly stack. That's greater than six of the top 10 teams in points! The key is that, because few users stacked teams like the Phillies and Mariners, they offered greater advantages than high-usage teams like the Dodgers, even with fewer points.

Another really interesting phenomenon we see is the presence of cheap stacks at the top of the leaderboard, as well as some expensive ones at the bottom. Marlins stacks, for example, led to 103.3 fantasy points—third-most in baseball. Does anyone think that the Marlins had the third-best offense in baseball last year? No, of course not, but they gave users tons of salary cap flexibility, which ultimately allowed them to roster better pitchers and score more points.

Thus, **we really need to be concerned about opportunity cost when considering stacks. It's not just about the upside of the stack, but also the flexibility it gives you in rostering specific types of pitchers**. The Marlins were one of my personal favorite teams to stack last year—the epitome of an antifragile offense. Similarly, we see offenses like the Red Sox, Yankees, Rangers, and White Sox all in the bottom six in points—likely the effect of a massive opportunity cost when it comes to spending on arms.

In addition to stacking data, I also have some numbers on the best teams to stack against.

Team Stacked Against	Avg Points	% GPPs Won	% of LUs which Won
Arizona	101.7	3.0%	0.23%
Colorado	101.5	4.8%	0.24%
Texas	101.4	4.3%	0.20%
Cincinnati	100.6	1.6%	0.20%
Chicago Cubs	100.3	1.2%	0.21%
Milwaukee	99.7	1.4%	0.32%
Toronto	98.2	1.9%	0.19%
Pittsburgh	97.8	2.3%	0.46%
Minnesota	97.7	1.4%	0.10%
Los Angeles	97.4	0.7%	0.19%

In terms of pure points, the Rockies actually checked in at No. 2 behind the Diamondbacks for points allowed. Texas was third. It's pretty interesting that two of the top three teams to stack against played in very hot temperatures (with the other having the obvious benefit of playing in thin air a mile above sea level).

Surprisingly, users had the most GPP success against the Pirates, winning 0.46 percent of all tournaments when stacking against Pittsburgh. I'm not really sure why that was the case, especially since the Pirates play in a stadium considered to be a pitcher's park.

In the data displaying the worst teams to stack against (in terms of pure points), we see more evidence of ownership being crucial to GPP success.

Team Stacked Against	Avg Points	% GPPs Won	% of LUs which Won
Tampa Bay	89.2	1.1%	0.25%
Oakland	90.5	0.7%	0.24%
Baltimore	90.9	2.2%	0.27%
Anaheim	91.3	1.7%	0.38%
Kansas City	91.9	0.3%	0.12%
Washington	92.2	1.0%	0.15%
Seattle	92.8	0.6%	0.09%
NY Yankees	93.8	0.6%	0.06%
San Francisco	94.7	0.2%	0.07%
Atlanta	95.3	1.9%	0.28%

Tampa Bay allowed the fewest points to opposing stacks last season, yet if you stacked against them, you had a better chance to win a tournament than versus all but two of the "most" favorable teams to stack against. We see a similar effect with Oakland, Baltimore, and especially Anaheim; users might have been scared to stack against the Angels (or it could be related to them playing on the West Coast), which ultimately led to a ton of GPP success for offenses facing the Angels, even if not a high level of fantasy production.

And finally, here's a look at stacking data based on the stadium in which the game was played.

Stadium Stacked	Avg Points	% GPPs Won	% of LUs which Won
Colorado	106.4	8.5%	0.34%
Cincinnati	101.3	1.1%	0.16%
Texas	100.9	3.9%	0.23%
Miami	100.2	1.8%	0.35%
Arizona	99.9	1.5%	0.17%
Washington	99.4	1.4%	0.23%
Minnesota	98.3	0.9%	0.11%
Pittsburgh	98.2	2.4%	0.34%
Milwaukee	97.7	2.7%	0.28%
Cleveland	97.4	1.2%	0.12%

Wow, shocking that the most points were scored at Coors Field. A huge number of points were scored in Colorado last season—and an outlying percentage of GPPs won—but **the actual success garnered by stacking at Coors actually wasn't tops in baseball**.

Actually, two stadiums that ranked in the bottom 10 in points allowed surpassed Colorado in terms of the percentage of lineups that won tournaments.

Stadium Stacked	Avg Points	% GPPs Won	% of LUs which Won
Tampa Bay	88.4	1.9%	0.18%
San Fran	88.5	1.1%	0.40%
Anaheim	91.2	1.1%	0.23%
Seattle	92.4	0.8%	0.13%
NY Yankees	92.7	2.5%	0.18%
Chi WS	93.0	1.0%	0.10%
NY Mets	93.1	1.1%	0.25%
Atlanta	93.3	1.3%	0.18%
San Diego	93.7	0.4%	0.16%
Houston	94.5	1.5%	0.42%

Users who rostered players in San Francisco and Houston had a better chance to win GPPs last year, despite a seriously reduced number of points. Again, this all comes down to ownership; everyone and their brother knows the Rockies (and their opponent) are a quality play at Coors Field.

I'm going to dive into the Coors Field effect in greater detail in one second, but first, take a look at the average number of home runs generated by the top stacks, opponents, and stadiums from last season.

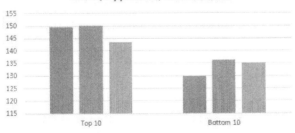

Average 2014 HR for Top/Bottom 10 Stacks, Opponents, and Stadiums

■ Stacks ■ Opponents ■ Stadiums

I told you chasing dongs is important. The teams and stadiums that were the most favorable to stack (or stack against) generated far more homers than the least favorable teams and stadiums.

Chicks dig the long-ball, and so do fantasy baseball nerds. Which means you guys have something in common, so feel free to use this data as a conversation-starter the next time you're at the bar. I picked up my girlfriend with detailed analysis of HR/FB rates, and the rest is history.

OH MY GOD THE ROCKIES ARE AT HOME!!!

Okay, back to Colorado. I mentioned that the Coors Field effect leads to the greatest number of points scored, by a mile, but that doesn't necessarily mean that you should automatically play teams at Coors.

But it doesn't mean you should fade them, either. Here's a look at some stacking data at Coors versus every other stadium.

Stadium Stacked	Avg Points	% GPPs Won	% of LUs which Won
Coors Field[1]	106.4	8.5%	0.34%
All Other Stadiums[2]	95.9	45.9%	0.21%

Far more points, as expected, but also more GPP success in terms of the percentage of lineups that won. Even though Coors Field is an obvious place to stack, I think it might still be underrated in terms of current ownership percentages. Don't forget this...

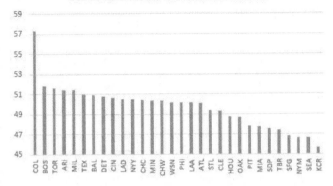

Pct of Total Bases at Home: 2011-2014

So we have a new rule: "Fade the very obvious plays in favor of second-tier stacks, unless the game is being played at Coors, in which case the ridiculously hitter-friendly conditions still aren't properly reflected in ownership." **I typically prefer to play the road team that's visiting Coors Field, as they seem to be less utilized than the Rockies**.

Also, notice that the total percentage of GPPs won by stacks in all stadiums was 54.4 percent. I defined a stack as four or more batters from the same team, which means that just under half of all DraftKings tournaments last season were won by non-stacks.

Most Rostered Players

Guys, I have some really bad news. This is the last section of data. Two more pieces and then adios. So sad.

First up is a list of the players who made it into the most winning 50/50 and GPP lineups last season.

50/50s	GPPs
Kole Calhoun	Mike Trout
Scooter Gennett	Miguel Cabrera
Mike Trout	Giancarlo Stanton
Brandon Moss	Jose Bautista
Miguel Cabrera	Kole Calhoun
Adrian Beltre	Adam Jones
Felix Hernandez	Josh Donaldson
Josh Donaldson	Jose Reyes
Stephen Strasburg	Anthony Rendon
Corey Dickerson	Nelson Cruz

Cool. Probably nothing useful here, but kind of interesting.

And here's a look at overall player usage broken down by team.

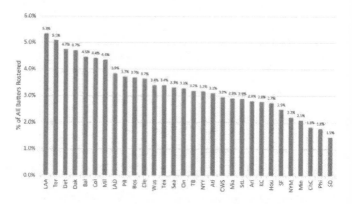

For me, there's nothing too surprising here other than perhaps the low usage of Miami, Houston, and San Francisco. Miami in particular, if you recall, was one of the most successfully stacked GPP teams last season. Some of that was inevitably due to the low ownership, but lineups with the Marlins also ranked third in fantasy points since they could be paired with elite arms.

I'll have my fair share of the top-owned stacks this year—the Angels, Blue Jays, Rockies, and the like—but it's the Miami-esque offenses that I believe are really underrated for use in GPPs.

> *"The time will come when diligent research over long periods will bring to light things which now lie hidden. There will come a time when our descendants will be amazed that we did not know things that are so plain to them."*
>
> *Seneca*

VII. The Jonathan Bales Chapter of General Daily Fantasy Baseball Heuristics for Daily Fantasy Baseball Players Who Can't Play Good and Who Wanna Learn to Do Other Stuff Good Too

"If you want to break the rules of grammar, first learn the rules of grammar."

Kurt Vonnegut

A heuristic is defined as "a technique for problem-solving and learning that finds a solution that, while not guaranteed to be optimal, speeds up the process of finding a satisfactory solution via mental shortcuts." Basically, a heuristic is a "rule of thumb"—not true in every situation, but good enough to improve overall decision-making.

A simple heuristic that could help NFL coaches is "Never punt on fourth down in opponent territory." The numbers are so incredibly against punting on almost every fourth down once a team crosses midfield (and many fourth down situations even in their own territory), yet we still see risk-averse coaches "playing it safe" by punting. Not going for it is the true risky play since it dramatically decreases expected points.

However, it's not like that heuristic, which is true in most situations, is an unbreakable rule. There are times when football games are no longer about point-maximization, wherein punting could decrease expected points but still improve a team's win probability.

But, as Kurt Vonnegut said, "If you want to break the rules of grammar, first learn the rules of grammar." I think this is a really important point that a lot of the every-situation-is-unique and stats-don't-tell-the-whole-story crowds miss; there are exceptions to every rule, but you're not going to have a lot of success if you're continually siding with those exceptions.

I think heuristics are particularly useful in daily fantasy baseball because of the lack of predictability in the game. If we could more accurately predict which batters would have huge games, for example, then it would make sense to more consistently break the general rule of "Save money on bats." The daily volatility in Major League Baseball makes the long-term trends—and the heuristics that are based off of them—more valuable.

Every rule is made to be broken, but if you don't know the rules, you can't successfully play the game.

Research Heuristics
1. Don't roster batters in games with a high probability of rain.
2. Don't use pitchers if there's any significant chance of a delay whatsoever.
3. Consider temperature, wind speed and direction, air pressure, and humidity when selecting players.
4. Use the Vegas lines as a proxy for fantasy production.

5. Target batters in games with a projected total above 9.5 runs.
6. Target pitchers if their team has a favorable moneyline and/or the opposing offense is projected poorly by Vegas.
7. Break down all statistics by handedness.
8. wOBA is the best offensive catch-all statistic, and ISO is best for representing power.
9. The two pitching stats you should weigh most heavily are SIERA and K/9.
10. Don't consider others' opinions until you've completed your own research.
11. Don't waste your time creating very specific MLB player projections, which are fragile.
12. You can use BvP for pitchers, occasionally, or to help predict ownership.
13. Leverage your significant other's uncanny intuition into PURE PROFIT.

League-Specific Heuristics

1. You shouldn't try to maximize points in either cash games or GPPs.
2. Your goal in cash games is to beat the average lineup as often as possible.
3. Your aim in tournaments is to increase your exposure to elite scores *and* the benefits you'll receive if your lineup scores a lot of points.
4. You should allocate a high percentage of your DraftKings salary cap to pitching in cash games *and* GPPs.
5. Stacking teammates is smart in cash games, too.

6. You should seek power from your bats and strikeouts from your arms, regardless of the league type.
7. You shouldn't avoid multi-entry 50/50s, which have a lower average score than single-entry.
8. Your GPP strategy shouldn't be to target the teams/players most likely to win that tournament (for anyone), but rather to field the combination of players that will maximize *your* probability of winning.

Batter Selection Heuristics

1. Right-handed batters are less pitcher-dependent than lefties (who struggle mightily as a whole versus southpaws).
2. Primarily left-handed stacks are more volatile than primarily right-handed stacks.
3. Most right-handed bats are better for cash games.
4. Avoid ground ball hitters as much as possible.
5. Target fly ball hitters against ground ball pitchers.
6. Fly ball hitters are less pitcher-dependent than ground ball hitters, and thus better for use in cash games.
7. Your batters should possess either the ability to go deep or the ability to steal bases.
8. The first key to projecting steals is first finding players who will get on base, which is more important than pitcher handedness.
9. Avoid base-stealers trying to run on the top catchers, like Yadier Molina.
10. Successful cash-game lineups generally acquire as many plate appearances as possible.

11. Successful tournament lineups balance plate appearances with power.
12. Using hitters at the bottom of the lineup is okay for GPPs if they're part of a high-upside offense.
13. Don't fade top-priced bats if they're obvious values.
14. Use BABIP, HR/FB, and other predictive stats to "buy low" on slumping players.
15. Offenses with extreme splits by handedness can offer more value than balanced offenses.
16. Some offenses don't have enough upside to consistently win GPPs.
17. Target away batters for safety in cash games.
18. Teams visiting Coors Field are still under-owned in GPPs.

Pitcher Selection Heuristics

1. Your first aim when selecting pitchers should be risk avoidance.
2. GB/FB and K/9 are the most consistent pitching stats.
3. Start both cash and GPP lineups by selecting low-risk pitchers with high-strikeout upside.
4. Consider K/9 for a pitcher's opponent, too.
5. Target ground ball pitchers as much as possible, specifically versus ground ball offenses.
6. Don't go cheap at pitcher if he doesn't have an attractive strikeout rate.
7. Use Vegas lines and props to help predict pitcher performance.
8. All batter research is directly applicable to pitchers, and vice versa.

9. Implement a "robust" pitcher selection strategy, i.e. try to "not fuck it up" more so than trying to hit the metaphorical home run.

Other Heuristics

1. Use data to confirm or debunk what you think you know; always be flexible in your beliefs and strategies.
2. Teams playing on the West Coast are generally underutilized in tournaments.
3. Players coming off of one game of above-average play are much more popular than those off of a below-average performance.
4. The easiest path to daily fantasy baseball success is to embrace randomness, not avoid it.
5. Randomness can ironically be very predictable because outliers regress toward the mean so predictably.
6. An antifragile approach to daily fantasy sports is one that loses small amounts consistently, but makes up for it with occasional massive profits.
7. Acknowledge your fallibility and you'll be in a better position.
8. Use science in daily fantasy sports to falsify your inaccurate beliefs and evolve as a player.

"The positive heuristic saves the scientist from being confused by the ocean of anomalies."

Imre Lakatos

VIII: Sample from "Daily Fantasy Pros Reveal Their Money-Making Secrets"

The following is an excerpt from my book Daily Fantasy Pros Reveal Their Money-Making Secrets in which I discussed the Vegas lines with Mirage88.

I'm a huge proponent of "stealing" research from Vegas by looking at their game lines, spreads, totals, prop bets, and so on. These are people who have millions of dollars on the line with each game, so creating an accurate line is important to them. It's not that we can't know that the Broncos are going to score a lot of points without looking to Vegas, but rather that the lines allow us to 1) quantify the effect and 2) do it in a really efficient way so we can spend precious research time elsewhere.

I spoke with Mirage88—one of daily fantasy's up-and-coming players—about his use of Vegas. Mirage88 is one of the smartest people I've spoken to about daily fantasy sports. He's also my favorite daily fantasy success story.

Within two weeks of learning about daily fantasy, Mirage88 qualified for a daily fantasy football championship and then won $25,000 just one month after that. A few months later, he went on a two-week heater that included a six-figure profit.

Rankings	Mirage88
Overall updates weekly on Thursday	
Overall Ranking	60th (43132.85)
TPOY Ranking	12th (13057.00)
Monthly Grinder Leaderboard	16th (2920.07)
NFL Grinder Leaderboard	26th (13937.53)
MLB Grinder Leaderboard	43rd (11142.31)
NBA Grinder Leaderboard	1616th (727.69)

Currently ranked in the top 30 in NFL, top 50 in MLB, and top 12 in TPOY, I'd argue that Mirage88 is one of the top 10 daily fantasy players in the world.

First, talk to me about the Vegas lines and how they're created.

I think it's important to understand how the Vegas lines are created, which then aids us in figuring out how useful they are. There's a perception that Vegas sets lines solely to get 50/50 action on each side of the bet. And to some degree they probably want that in many situations since they'll guarantee themselves profit just from the juice (the commission they charge to play). But what happens is people will sometimes use that as a reason that Vegas shouldn't be used in projections, saying something like "Oh, they just care about whatever popular opinion might be and just getting in the middle of that."

The problem with that is that there are a lot of sharp bettors out there with a lot of money, so if Vegas indeed produces a line to equalize bets but it's weak, those sharps are just going to pound that bet and Vegas will be in a really poor situation in terms of expected value.

So the way I like to think about Vegas is that it's really where the most risk is in terms of projecting any player results—at least the most financial risk from one entity making projections, anyway. So if Vegas posts a poor line—let's say they post a total that's way too low—then all of a sudden anyone who can bet on that who is relatively sharp will just start hitting the over, and Vegas will realize that the bet isn't really balanced.

Vegas will compensate for that by moving the total up to get more action on the under. That's fine, but then there's this area in the middle which was over the initial line but under the new line movement bet that's now a really bad place for Vegas. If the game ends up in that spot, they could theoretically lose a whole lot of bets to sharps who bet the original over, but at the same time lose late bets that came in on the under when the total was higher.

Vegas doesn't want to put themselves in that position where they can be arbitraged, so it's really important for them to create an accurate line from the start. Even if they don't guarantee a profit by getting equal money on each side, they can limit their downside—their risk of ruin—by making the line accurate. They really don't want to be in a situation where they set a bad line that moves a whole lot and they could potentially lose their share on both sides of a bet.

So to be clear, Vegas needs to set accurate lines to not only ensure that they get equal money on both sides, which they will, but so that *actual results* fall on both sides of the bet 50 percent of the time over the long run as well. It's okay if they get 70 percent of action on one side of a bet and 30 percent on the other if, over time, the actual results are falling half over and half under—meaning Vegas is setting accurate lines.

Ultimately, making accurate lines is just a safer way for Vegas to make money than trying to predict public opinion, especially when there are sharks out there who might not agree with public opinion. Vegas has a very clear financial incentive to make accurate lines, and they do. So that's my little rant on why we can trust the lines and why the idea that all Vegas wants is to balance bets is false.

How do you personally use the lines in your daily fantasy projections?

I personally use the lines whenever there aren't time constraints. So if the lines come out a couple hours before a game, that's a little difficult to fit into a model to make projections and still be able to create lineups and all that. But any Vegas line that comes out early enough that I think relates to something that I'm trying to project gets put into my model.

In football, I'm usually looking at projected totals the most. The easiest way to use over/unders in football is to look at the total and the spread and calculate the projected total for each team. You can do that pretty easily on your own, but I go to RotoGrinders for that info to get it really quickly.

Once I have the total for each team, I look at some historical scoring rates—what percentage of scoring has typically gone to each position for certain teams. So let's say we're looking at the Packers and the Giants, who Vegas has projected at 24 points each. By looking at historical scoring, we'd see that we should project Aaron Rodgers with more touchdowns than Eli Manning just because Green Bay scores a higher percentage of touchdowns to field goals, and Rodgers also accounts for a much higher percentage of the Packers' scores than Manning for the Giants, even with the same projected points.

You need to be careful there, too, because there can be a lot of turnover in the NFL, so things change. For example, the Giants have a new offensive coordinator and an entirely new offensive philosophy, so that data on how their touchdowns are usually allocated might change. For the Packers, on the other hand, we can pretty much assume the same scoring rates since not much has changed for them in terms of coaching or personnel.

I think that's also a good example of projections sometimes being really scientific and other times being more of an art. With Green Bay, I'd be more likely to rely on the numbers; I can look back at however many years the same sort of scheme was in place and say, "Okay, 20 percent of touchdowns go to Jordy Nelson, 35 percent go to running backs, and so on."

You can actually do the same sort of thing when projecting kickers, looking at a combination of the line and then what percentage of points the kicker has produced, assuming there haven't been giant shifts in offensive philosophy or personnel.

After that, you still need to adjust for other factors, specifically the opponent. Maybe the Packers' wide receivers account for 50 percent of all touchdowns, but they're facing a defense that has really short cornerbacks who get picked on in the red zone, so they allow 65 percent of touchdowns to opposing receivers. Then you'd expect an even greater rate of the scoring to come from Nelson & Co.

But that's the general idea behind what I do to at least get a baseline projection.

Do you study only totals? How about player props?

I don't use props, but not because they aren't useful. They have the same predictive power of any other number put out by Vegas. The main reason I don't use the props, though, is that they tend to come out pretty late in the week, so that doesn't leave much time to get them into my projection model. I can pretty much calculate projected touchdowns, especially, from using the total and past scoring rates alone, so I can do that earlier in the week when the lines are posted. That's a way to basically get most of the way to creating the props without the props actually being released.

The other thing is that I think there's something to be said for simplicity in a model. It's really important to understand everything that goes into your model and how it affects the projection, and sometimes it doesn't make sense to have all these little minute details coming in from 50 different sources.

So I don't know if I'd make player props a major component of my model even if they did come out earlier in the week, just because it's important to understand what's driving your model in order to improve it. If you have a bunch of different components in your model and it doesn't work, it's going to be really difficult for you to figure out why and make a change. A huge part of being a profitable daily fantasy player is about improvement, so you need to know where your projections are coming from and how they can be enhanced.

What percentage of players do you think look at the lines? How does that affect their worth?

I'd say that almost all high-volume players are looking at the lines in some form or another. Some put more weight into them than others, but if you're a successful daily fantasy player, I'd be surprised if you aren't looking at the lines at all.

In terms of the overall player pool, though, I think it's probably still a tiny percentage, which adds to their worth. I think there's a ton of value in using the lines, especially in cash games, because in head-to-head or 50/50 matchups, for example, you're just looking to figure out the most likely thing that's going to happen and use that to beat the average player. Using the Vegas lines is a really accurate way to accomplish that.

In cash games, I think Vegas can really help with your own projections. In tournaments, I think the biggest value from the lines comes in using them as a prediction market for ownership. So the higher the over/under on a game, the more player utilization there will be in those games. Even if the general public isn't using the Vegas lines, they still have a sense of which games are going to be high-scoring, so Vegas can act as confirmation of where there's going to be heavy player usage.

That's important because, unlike in cash games, it's important to have a unique lineup in tournaments. So if there's a game that's an outlier in terms of the projected total, just way ahead of everything else, it's kind of hard to recommend players from that game because they're going to be so popular. That doesn't mean I never use players from the highest-projected game in tournaments, but if I do, I need to create some elements within my roster that I think won't be as common elsewhere. It's not that you can't win by using all highly utilized players, but just that it can improve your tournament odds by adding at least some contrarian elements into your lineup when you otherwise go with the chalk.

How do you know when to go against Vegas and when to play the chalk?

I think this is one of the aspects of daily fantasy that's still more art than science. My general philosophy, at least in tournaments, is to take the best possible players who I think won't be really popular choices for the rest of the daily fantasy community.

So let's say that the Broncos are projected way ahead of everyone else in a given week and also have some attractive salaries, to the point that we pretty much know Denver players are going to see extremely high usage. In that situation, I tend to look at the next few highest-projected teams and then try to think about which ones won't be very popular—maybe they aren't getting a lot of buzz or they play in a small market—and try to target players on those teams. Even if they aren't projected quite as high as the Broncos, you make up for that by creating a lineup that doesn't resemble many others, whereas maybe 30 percent of the field is creating very similar Broncos-centric lineups.

So in a way, I'm still playing chalk in that I want them to be projected to score a lot of points, but just that I care about how popular I think a team's players will be, too. It's also an experience sort of thing where you'll get better as you play in more tournaments.

Another time when I like to go against the top-projected team is when I see certain players on poor teams come out as really good values. Maybe there will be a case where a team isn't projected to score that many points, but their quarterback and top receiver are likely to account for a huge percentage of their overall yards and touchdowns. I love to target those situations because I can still get value with the projections, but I know the public won't be on them because they aren't projected that high as a team. So again, I'm just using the Vegas totals as a proxy for daily fantasy ownership.

What percentage of your model is composed of Vegas-based data?

It depends on the sport. I think Vegas is a really powerful tool, but it's just one of many projections I use. One of my goals is to find as many projections from as many smart people as I can find and just aggregate them. So I make projections myself, I use Vegas, I look at sites that I trust, and I factor all of those into my model.

As long as I think the projections are coming via a quality process, I love to just aggregate a whole bunch of information to factor out as much bias as I can, whether it's my own personal biases or individual site bias. So Vegas might be just one-fourth or one-fifth of my model, although I do change the weight I place on each source as I see fit.

The bigger picture is that I really am a huge proponent of aggregating data from a few trusted sources. I think it's the easiest way to build an accurate projection—the "wisdom of the crowd"—and Vegas is a big component of that, although certainly not the only source I rely on.

Which aspects of daily fantasy projections aren't priced into the Vegas lines?

For the most part, I think they're going to do a really good job of capturing most relevant statistics. Again, there's so much money on the line that it's hard to believe there's a really powerful predictive measure that they aren't considering.

But if something isn't priced in, it's factors that they aren't aware of when they set the line. The biggest example of that is weather. Vegas posts lines early in the week without full knowledge of weather conditions days down the line, so that's something that certainly affects player production but won't be a major component of the early lines. The classic example is a 2013 game between the Eagles and Lions that had a huge over/under that was posted on Monday—a total that needed to be adjusted considerably because forecasts were calling for a massive blizzard during the game.

It's not just Vegas that doesn't initially account for weather, though. Most projections aren't going to have weather as much of a component to start just because we can't really know how the weather is going to look during a game days in advance. So weather is a really, really important aspect of projections to monitor.

Injuries are another aspect of daily fantasy production that might not be priced into the Vegas lines when they first come out. Let's say Aaron Rodgers is questionable but expected to play in a given game, but just before kickoff he's ruled out. Vegas might have set the total as if Rodgers were going to play, but that's going to be altered significantly if he can't go, which will of course extend to projections for his teammates as well.

Do you ever study line movements? How might those be useful?

I don't think the lines move all that much in most cases because, like I said, Vegas generally posts strong lines. When it does move a lot, I think that's really good evidence of strong public perception in one way or the other.

That has the most use in tournaments because if you see the public strongly moving in one direction, that's probably a reason for you to move in the other. I think you want to avoid following the public when a line moves because basically that's a case where the general populace likes a team more than Vegas. We can usually equate the general betting populace to the average daily fantasy player, so when a line moves a lot in a particular direction, it's a decent sign that a lot of users are going to be higher on certain players than Vegas would be—and thus their ownership will be higher than it should be.

Whether or not I target players in a game that moves a lot depends on which direction it moves. If a game moves up, it means that there's probably going to be heavy usage on players that Vegas doesn't like as much as the public, and that's a situation to fade. If a line moves down, it means Vegas is higher on a team than the public, and that's a situation to target because you can get value on players who are unlikely to be heavily utilized. That's not a hard-and-fast rule that I use—again, it's still more of an art than science at this point—but it's a good rule-of-thumb regarding value and ownership percentages.

Tell us about a time when you successfully leveraged Vegas.

I have an example from MLB. After completing my baseball projections for the day, I ranked my top teams to stack simply by sorting average fantasy points per batter on each team. I saw that the Cubs were the sixth-highest total out of 20 teams in my model, but had the third-lowest projected total in Vegas. The downside of that over/under was already included as an input in my projection, so I felt good going with the Cubs despite the low projected total.

I also got a sense that the opposing pitcher, Tyler Lyons, was going to be highly owned based on industry articles and podcasts recommending him. Given that Lyons isn't an ace pitcher and my model had batters with a decent projection against him, it was a perfect opportunity. I got to stack a low-ownership team while getting double the value, as the poor performance of the opposing pitcher would sink a lot of my opponents' teams. Regardless of outcome, that's the type of shot I love taking in big tournaments because when they work, they win big. In that case, I had three Cubs stacks finish 1-2-3 due to the contrarian nature of the picks.

CSURAM88's Analysis

I'm a huge proponent of using the Vegas lines for information because they've proven to be so accurate, and Mirage88 did a great job of explaining why that's the case. One thing the lines allow me to do which is different from some other players is target teams over players.

That is, I look at the Vegas lines and use those to help me figure out which teams are going to be able to score a lot in a game. Then, I try to predict which players on that team are going to be the main beneficiaries of that.

Overall, though, I am 100 percent a Vegas-based daily fantasy player; I use the lines as a very strong foundation for my projections and lineups, and I don't think there's a more efficient and useful way to go about playing daily fantasy. In addition to game totals, I look at team totals, line movement, player props—anything I can get my hands on.

Postface

A 'postface' is a real thing. I'm a VERY SERIOUS AUTHOR, so I think I'd know. I started using them a few books ago when I Google'd "opposite of preface."

So I guess this is where I say goodbye. But it's not really goodbye, because I'm sure I'll see you on DraftKings this MLB season—getting second place in all the big tournaments behind me.

I was going to write out a longer postface, but I'm really hungry and I have all of the stuff to make fish tacos, sooooo...yeahhh.

Don't forget your free stuff.

DraftKings

Daily Fantasy Sports for Cash

In addition to a free game, you'll immediately get a 100% deposit bonus up to $600 if you sign up and deposit on DraftKings.

10% Off Everything On My Site (Books, DFS Packages, Etc)

If you want to purchase my Daily Fantasy Baseball Package or any of the books in my Fantasy Sports for Smart People book series, you can do that at FantasyFootballDrafting.com. If you head over there, use the coupon code "Smart10" at checkout to get 10% off your entire order.

Free Issue of RotoAcademy—My Daily Fantasy Sports Training School

Finally, I'm also giving away a free issue—12 lessons—from my daily fantasy sports training school RotoAcademy. I founded RotoAcademy to bridge the gap between the average daily fantasy sports player and the game's elite. My goal is to teach you the tricks of the trade—and give you all kinds of unique data on what's actually winning leagues (like what's in this book)—to help you become a profitable DFS player.

Download the free lessons at RotoAcademy.com/free-download/ or visit RotoAcademy.com/about-faq/ to learn more.

And I can't forget, big shout out to rapper DMX, who has been instrumental in the creation of my books. D – Your insights on the false dichotomy between randomness and predictability were inspiring, dog.

Made in the USA
Charleston, SC
02 April 2015